LOOK BIG

LOOK BIG

**And other tips for
surviving animal encounters
of all kinds**

RACHEL LEVIN

illustrations by Jeff Östberg

TEN SPEED PRESS
California | New York

CONTENTS

Introduction: It's a Wild World 7

Alligators 10

Ants 13
  / Ants in the Minivan
    by McKenzie Funk 14

Bats 17

Bears (Black, Grizzly,
and Brown) 18
  / Grizzlies in Alaska
    by Peter Fish 22

Bed Bugs 24
  / Bed Bugs on the Mind
    by Brooke Borel 27

Bees, Wasps, and Hornets 28

Bison 31

Black Widow Spiders 32

Bobcats 34

Cockroaches 37
  / Cockroaches in New York
    (of Course) by Bonnie Tsui 38

Cows 40

Coyotes 43
  / Coyotes in My Face
    by Chris Colin 45

Crows 46

Deer 51
  / Deer in the Suburbs
    by Vanessa Hua 52

Dogs 55

Donkeys 56

Dust Mites 59

Elephant Seals 60

Foxes 63

Fruit Flies 64

Geese 67

Horses 68

Jaguars 71

Jellyfish 72

Lice 74

Mice 77
/ Mice in the Backseat
  by Samin Nosrat 78
Moose 81
Mosquitoes 82
Mountain Lions 84
Opossums 87
Owls (Great Horned) 89
Pigeons 90
Porcupines 92
Rabbits 95
/ Bunnies in the Backyard
  by Rebecca Flint Marx 96
Raccoons 98
/ Raccoons in the Kitchen
  by Peter Orner 100
Rats 102
/ Rats in the Bedroom
  by Diana Kapp 107
Rattlesnakes 108

Seagulls 110
Sea Urchins 113
Sharks 114
Sheep 118
Skunks 121
Squirrels 122
Stingrays 125
Ticks 126
Turkeys 129
Whales 130
Wild Boars 132
Wolves 136
Woodpeckers 139

Animals from Most to
Least Deadly 140
Acknowledgments 141
Index 142

INTRODUCTION:
IT'S A WILD WORLD

One gray winter day, I was cross-country skiing, head down, through the snowy woods outside Breckenridge, Colorado, when luckily I looked up. Blocking my path, less than twenty feet ahead, was a wise, old, bearded giant, like out of a Roald Dahl story.

He just stood there, this ginormous four-legged creature, poised and upright between the evergreens, quietly staring. I stared back. And almost instinctually, foolishly, I whipped out my phone to snap a picture. But then my natural-born instincts kicked in. Wait a minute. This isn't the Big Friendly Giant—it's a Big-Ass Moose. What are the rules when you see a moose—up close? I had no idea. So, of course, I did what you're not supposed to do when you see a moose: I turned my back and glided away.

"Please don't follow me," I kindly requested, aloud.

"A moose wouldn't follow you," my husband later told me; I was home, safe, on the couch with a beer. "It would charge you."

Charge me! But it had looked so calm. So gentle! Who knew that a moose, when startled, could be as dangerous as a grizzly? I didn't.

And even though I love to trail run solo around Northern California, I can never *quite* remember what to do if I come across a mountain lion. Or if I bump into a mama grizzly with her cubs while hiking in, say, British Columbia where, personally, I like to yell "HI BEARS!" every twenty seconds, so I don't. Or what about all those black bears in Yosemite? On one backcountry camping trip, two took down a jumbo bag of M&Ms hanging from a tree while we slept.

Meanwhile, back home in San Francisco, a small nation of ants often takes over our kitchen; raccoons relentlessly rummage through the trash; and once, a pair of skunks having sex on our front stoop wouldn't budge. Oh, and my kids had lice, twice.

It's an increasingly wild world out there. Wildlife and humans have long been at odds, in ways both big and small. But as we continue to build 4,000-square-foot homes where forests once stood and pile into cities (predator-free, all-you-can-eat buffets for the animals that follow), our lives are intersecting more and more. It turns out, animals appreciate the ease of urban and suburban life as much as we do. They're thriving. We're cowering. And it's getting a little out of hand for everyone involved.

Rats are having pizza parties in Philadelphia. Bears are climbing into kitchens in the Sierra. Coyotes are casing playgrounds in Los Angeles. Mountain lions are mauling dogs in Denver backyards. And, in Ocean City, New Jersey, seagulls are swiping pizza and popcorn right out of people's hands.

The thing is, though, people aren't acting any better.

Last year, researcher Vincenzo Penteriani concluded that nearly half of attacks by large carnivores—including bears, coyotes, and cougars—are associated with "unnecessarily risky human behavior," also known as blatantly stupid human behavior.

Remember the tourists in Yellowstone National Park who stuffed a baby bison in the trunk of their car because they thought it looked cold? (It later died due to their interference.) There was a family in Pennsylvania who put a leash on a bear cub and had it prance around their yard. And a Florida woman was known to nurse abandoned raccoons. (Yeah.)

These are good examples of *what not to do* when you encounter a baby bison or bear cub or raccoon. Here's another thing you should not do: take a selfie or snuggle up. (Go online to check out how close Carrie Underwood got to her new friend "Moosh" in the name of Instagram.)

Clearly, we humans need a reminder of *what to do* when we encounter all sorts of animals; whether we're in Banff or Boulder, the Bob Marshall Wilderness or Brooklyn. It may not be fair, but it's on us—we're the humans. We've invented driverless cars and robots that cook crab bisque; it shouldn't be *that* hard to figure out how to peacefully coexist with coyotes.

After all, we've learned to live in congested environments with each other (for the most part). "We don't have to love animals," says Colin Jerolmack, a sociologist at NYU with a thing for pigeons. "We just have to ignore them, the same way we do when we're smashed up against someone's armpit on the subway." At least, ignore *some* animals. For example, stop feeding bears (see page 18)! Stop dressing squirrels in tiaras (see page 122)! Just let them do their wildlife thing. Other animals require a more . . . proactive approach.

What we, as humans, are supposed to do when we encounter an animal depends on which animal it is. There are recommended ways to respond in every situation. It's just so hard to keep it all straight: Look big! Look small! Run. Don't run! Fight back. Play dead! Wait, no, don't play dead. Spray Tabasco sauce. Sprinkle baby powder. Pay $800 to a "salon" called Hair Fairies (no, don't—that's ridiculous).

The tips are all out there, somewhere—outdated, updated, posted at the trailhead or at the beach, buried on nps.gov or on the back of your bottle of bug repellent. I thought it'd be handy to have everything in one place: an authoritative, all-in-one guide to dealing with North America's most feared or frustrating animals. As a semi-neurotic urbanite who loves the outdoors— just not coming face-to-face with every creature in it—writing this book was like a form of exposure therapy, an attempt to work it all out for myself, so that the next time I'm hiking in the Sawtooth National Forest or running at Point Reyes National Seashore or picking nits out of my daughter's hair, I'll feel a little more prepared.

I mean, I'll still freak out. But at least I'll have all the info. And now, so will you.

ALLIGATORS

/ *Also known as: Gators.*

FOUND Lurking in lakes, rivers, swamps, golf course ponds throughout the southeastern United States, and—don't forget—Disney World. Lost pet alligators are occasionally spotted on New York City streets, too.

SIZE As long as a balance beam; as heavy as a grand piano.

SOUNDS A growly hiss, or a slow, deep burp, like a car having startup trouble.

"Every body of freshwater in Florida has alligators in it," says Ken Rice, director of the U.S. Geological Survey, Wetland and Aquatic Research Center in Gainesville. "You just don't always see them."

But a gator prowls, eyes peeking above the surface, ginormous jaw poised for whatever crosses its path: fish, frogs, turtles, each other, a deer if it's lucky. It's very rare for an alligator to bother a human being. But it happens. "They'll eat anything they come in contact with," says Rice. *Anything*. And anyone.

So, when in alligator-land, avoid swimming, even wading, especially at dawn or dusk; no dangling your legs off a boat, no making noise; and never, *ever* *feed* an alligator. As Rice puts it, "Best to just stay out of the water—and out of their way."

If for some insane reason you don't. . . .

WHAT TO DO

Run—zigzag, straight line, doesn't matter. Alligators might be the only predators in the world you'd have a shot at beating in a race. Though they rarely pursue on land, around water, stay alert. Alligators ambush. They latch on to prey, roll it underwater until drowned and dead, then toss it back like a tequila shot. Which means that adult humans aren't easy eating.

Put up a decent fight, and the alligator might decide to ditch you. "They prefer not to contend with violently struggling prey," says Allan Woodward of Florida's Fish and Wildlife Research Institute. "Scream. Splash. Kick. Sure, *try* and punch the snout or gouge out the eyes," says Woodward. "No guarantees, but it has worked before."

BY THE NUMBERS

1.3 million: Number of alligators in Florida.

380: Unprovoked attacks on people since 1948.

24: People killed by alligators since 1973.

$100: Cost to wrestle a live alligator at Gators Reptile Park in Colorado.

DISCONCERTING THOUGHT

For every ant or two you spot on your counter, says Fisher, there's an "infinite amount" nesting in your walls.

DISCONCERTING FACT

Humans have 100 billion brain cells. Ants have 250,000 brain cells. Which means a colony of 1 million ants has 250 billion brain cells. (No wonder we're having trouble outsmarting them.)

ANTS

/ *Also known as: Carpenter ants, black ants, Argentine ants, pharaohs, and, of course, queens.*

FOUND Everywhere but Antarctica, and especially in your house, when it's raining outside.

SIZE Like aspirin, tiny but mighty.

Lay's once came up with a clever slogan for its potato chips: "Bet you can't eat just one!" It was a good slogan because it's true. Who eats just one potato chip? Similarly, ants: you never see just one, especially if you leave crumbs of potato chips lying around.

Ants weasel their way in through cracks and take over, marching through your house like they own the place—which, until you get rid of them, they pretty much do.

Bottles of honey, boxes of cereal, bathtubs, countertops, laptops!—nothing is sacred. Two ants were once discovered in the bristles of a Superman toothbrush, after brushing. Even Superman is powerless in the face of ants.

WHAT TO DO

There are lots of home remedies. Most tend to involve lemon juice or white vinegar or little tubs of Tabasco sauce. "No one has ever studied what really works," says Brian Fisher, entomologist at California Academy of Sciences. Until now.

Last year, his team launched a citizen science project, urging people with ant-infested homes everywhere to try DIY solutions and send in their results. There's no winner yet, but so far the strongest contenders seem to be lemon and cinnamon. Why? Fisher and his team are still figuring that out. But the rest of those cockamamy concoctions? "Probably bogus," he predicts.

Calling an exterminator can be helpful, except for the cost and chemicals. The best plan of attack is to caulk ants' entryways, says Fisher. Use Vaseline if you have to.

And if nothing else works, according to the 5,000 impassioned posts on Amazon, TERRO Liquid Ant Baits (the superstar of ant traps) will . . . until next season.

ANTS IN THE MINIVAN

By McKenzie Funk, journalist and author of
Windfall: The Booming Business of Global Warming

There are some things a person doesn't see coming in life. For me, it was maturity, a 2008 Toyota Sienna, and ants.

Adulthood arrived in a tsunami of marriage, homeownership, kids, and responsibilities that had me rooted in Seattle. Suddenly, instead of interviewing soldiers abroad, I found myself embattled at home, with an overpriced, underskilled contractor who fled, leaving behind a big mess and an even bigger blue Shop-Vac.

The ants, though, stayed; they'd come with the house. We'd gotten used to them. They marched in twos and smelled like lemongrass, squashed. But then they came for the minivan.

A minivan is no man's dream. But, one spring day, it was my nightmare.

The automatic door slid open to reveal my kid's car seat quivering. I looked closer. Ants? I lifted it up. They were *everywhere*: running up my arms, onto my head, into the upholstery, flooding the floor mats—thousands and thousands and thousands of ants.

An ecologist could explain why they chose to nest here, in warm cushions covered in apple chunks and Cheerios. But ecology is never a primary concern in times of combat.

Horrified, hands gloved in ants, I threw the car seats on the lawn, ripped out the bucket seats, and froze. Then I remembered the Shop-Vac, sitting idle for six years. The ants didn't stand a chance. I aimed the tube and sucked clean every crack, every seam.

Satisfaction. Power. Some soldiers are attracted to the machinery of war, to the weapons in their hands. Suddenly, crouched inside a beige minivan, holding the world's most powerful vacuum, I understand.

BATS

/ Also known as: "Flying rats,"
which is totally incorrect.
But they are flying mammals,
the only ones in the world.

FOUND Roosting by the millions in caves and chimneys, and hanging upside down from rafters everywhere.

SIZE Weighs as much as a baseball, with a foot-long wingspan.

SOUNDS Squeaky-screechy. Creepy.

Bats eat bugs—lots of bugs—and thank god they do or we'd be overrun and our ecosystem would be totally out of whack. The only time bats seem to bother us is on summer nights. They swoop down when we're having drinks on the deck, or silently bite us in our sleep, or occasionally get under foot, like the time a woman padding around her kitchen accidentally squished a bat between her toes (ew).

A bat bite wouldn't be the worst thing in the world—except for a little disease called rabies. Only about 1 percent of bats carry it, but still, bat encounters are the most common way for people to get rabies in the United States, according to the Centers for Disease Control and Prevention.

WHAT TO DO

Used to be, you only panicked if you saw tiny teeth marks on your skin, or were feeling dizzy or delirious. But after multiple cases of people unknowingly contracting rabies just from being *in the same room* as a bat, experts now agree: get tested, no matter what.

How do you get the bat the hell out of your bedroom, though? That's tricky. Leave it to the pros. Then again, they're not always around at 3 a.m. So, if need be, pull on leather gloves. (Don't have leather gloves lying around in summer or ever? No matter.) Take a plastic container that has a lid, approach slowly, and place the open container over the bat. Slide the lid under and, quickly, duct tape it shut. Don't kill it; that's illegal. Or, says a salesman at A-Team pest control in Los Angeles: "Just open a window—it'll find its way out."

No, bats are not after your hair, just the bugs flying around it. / One brown bat devours 1,000 mosquitoes in an hour. / Bat populations are declining, and a disease called white-nose syndrome is making it worse. So don't hate bats—as horrid as they may seem, we need them.

BLACK BEARS

/ *Also known as:* Ursus americanus.

FOUND From the Berkshires to Banff.

SIZE As big as a sofa.

GRIZZLY BEARS, BROWN BEARS

/ *Also known as:* Ursus arctos horribilis *(which is fitting).*

FOUND Alaska and Western Canada, Montana, Idaho, and Wyoming, with a few wandering in Washington.

SIZE Two to five times as heavy as your refrigerator.

It's awe inspiring, if terrifying, to see bears in the wild. It's also rather jarring to watch them crawl up the carpeted stairs of a ski condo while a guy hiding in the closet films it on his phone, then posts it on YouTube.

There are countless home videos like these online of bears where they shouldn't be: climbing over a car windshield while a baby screams in the backseat; throwing a pool party in Conneticut, which was cute, in a NIMBY kind of way. There was also a recent incident at Lake Tahoe, not online, unfortunately: a tray of pot brownies, just out of the oven, left cooling on the windowsill while everyone went out for a walk. When the people returned, they found that the bear, like Goldilocks, had eaten them all up.

Encounters with black bears are on the rise, says Ann Bryant, director of the Lake Tahoe–based BEAR League. "Twenty years ago, we'd get five calls a day; now we get two hundred," she says: there are more tourists, more locals living among the bears—then leaving windows open, food out, trashcans filled—and never learning how to properly live with them.

"Fifty percent of the time, we coach idiots," says Bryant. Like the dad who smeared peanut butter on his toddler's nose, then waited for a bear to lick

CONTINUED

it off (photo op, he'd explained) or the dude who left a cookie trail leading from his backyard to his couch because he thought it'd be fun to, you know, film a bear eating cookies while watching TV.

Please don't feed the bears! When they get too used to humans, they become a danger to themselves and us.

WHAT TO DO

In a heavily human place like Tahoe or Whistler, if a black bear is on your turf (deck, driveway, campground), it's simple, says Bryant. Be inhospitable. Clap, stomp, pound the window, yell. It'll flee. Squirt guns, beach balls, small stones (thrown at its butt) help scare it off, too. "Black bears are big chickens," she promises.

However, if you see a black bear or grizzly in the wild, on its own turf, it's more complicated. Be respectful, a good guest. The number-one rule, according to Dan LeGrandeur of Alberta-based Bear Scare: Stay calm (uh, okay). Don't scream or turn your back. DO NOT RUN; it will chase you (bears can motor up to 35 mph). Give it space. Say hello, out loud, in your most soothing yoga teacher voice— "Hi, bear. I'm human. Get the hell out of here, please," while slooowly backing away in the direction from which you came.

It's not about whether a bear is black or brown (and black bears can be brown, by the way), but how a bear is behaving, says LeGrandeur. "Read its signals."

It's either scared and asking you to go away (defensive) or wants to kill you and eat you (predatory). No pressure, but you need to figure that out fast.

Defensive bear behavior: Ears back, paws swatting, jaw clacking, huffing. Black bear cubs may climb a tree.

Your behavior: Retreat gradually while turned sideways and avoiding eye contact. Appear as unthreatening as you know you are.

Predatory bear behavior: Ears forward, head up, staring at you, quietly stalking.

Your behavior: Look big. Lock eyes. Shout. Throw stuff. Be intimidating; let it know who's, supposedly, boss.

There's a good chance the bear will leave. If it doesn't and charges? "%#@&." If it's defensive—most are—it's bluffing. Probably. "At that point, it's a hope and a prayer," admits LeGrandeur.

"Every muscle in your body is telling you otherwise, but DO NOT RUN." Instead, stand your ground and bust out the bear spray—98 percent of people who use it (properly) are unscathed. Comforting.

If a bear lays its paws on you . . .

Mama black bear or mama grizzly defending her cubs: Play dead.

Male black bear: Fight back, usually.

Male grizzly: It depends. Is the bear defensive? Play dead. Predatory? Fight for your life.

Black bear population: At 650,000 and counting.
/ Grizzly population: Only 1,800 left in the
Lower 48, but tens of thousands in Alaska and
British Columbia. / Bears eat 25,000 calories
a day . . . and only one person a year.

GRIZZLIES IN ALASKA

By Peter Fish, writer and editor focused on the American West

---

I assumed I'd signed up for some kind of package tour, as tourists do. I envisioned fellow nature lovers, a perky guide, bear-emblazoned tote bags. But when I got to the tiny seaplane, I was told, no, it was just me, dropped off on an island, by myself, for the entire day. Unless, weather. And the plane couldn't get back until the next day or the next.

I spent the forty-minute flight brooding on these possibilities. Then I brooded on the "bear safety" pamphlet: Hike in groups. (Too late.) Always let the bears know you're there. (Did anyone tell them I was coming?) Sing or talk loudly. (Sing?) Never run.

Wading on shore, I waved as the plane took off. Crooning Katy Perry's "California Gurls," I tramped toward the creek.

And then they appeared: a cinnamon-colored mammoth sow and her two brown cubs, the mother lumbering, babies bounding behind; then more, who left and returned. Commandeering the stream, massive clawed paws scooping salmon, biting in, leftovers plopping into the water.

I felt amazement, awe. And as a member of the race that has driven grizzlies to the brink of extinction, guilt. Powerful feelings. Turns out, though, you can't feel powerful feelings for ten hours, especially in a cold drizzle.

I was getting hungry—I hadn't brought food, for obvious reasons. Were the bears tiring of the salmon and looking at me? What if they charged? *Never run.* What was I doing out here, alone?

At dusk, I hiked back, Katy Perry more of a mutter now. The seaplane was late. But at least it picked me up.

BED BUGS

/ Also known as: Nightriders.

FOUND Tucked into mattresses and more, especially in summer.

SIZE An apple seed or a lentil, little but visible.

Bed bug is a misnomer. They're not just found in beds. In motel rooms, apartments, and multimillion-dollar homes, yes—but also in theater seats, taxis, the spines of popular library books.

And they're on the rise everywhere, according to a recent "Bugs Without Borders" survey. Manhattan hotels alone have seen a 44 percent year-over-year increase in bed-bug complaints. Once they hitch a ride into your house on luggage or clothes, it's nearly impossible to get the bloodsuckers to leave. That's what they do, by the way; they suck your blood—and you don't even feel it. They just leave itchy welts and then squirrel away to digest, have sex, and lay eggs until they crawl back for more. It's an all-consuming battle that has driven people to insomnia, PTSD, and divorce.

WHAT TO DO

Put pest control on speed dial and then ransack like a detective searching for evidence, emptying dressers, nightstands, and closets. Bed bugs hide behind headboards and mirrors, on carpets and couches. Scour every crevice and then declutter like you're Kondo on cold brew, and just keep vacuuming. Swap your wooden bed for steel. They can't climb metal or bathtubs. (Go ahead: get in and curl up.) Wash and dry everything on high heat, seal the rest of your stuff in Ziploc Big Bags (for up to a year according to the EPA), and toss whatever you can. This is no time for nostalgia.

Trained dogs can find the bed bugs if you can't ("Sherlock Hounds," as one company calls them). The PackTite Closet Bed Bug Heater System sounds like it helps, but $800 for a product that promises to roast bedbugs right off your shoes? Maybe just buy a new pair.

Bed bugs can live eighteen months without feeding. Sure, you could move out for a bit, but they'll still be there when you get back. / Of those people bitten by bed bugs, 70 percent react to the bites; 30 percent don't. *You might not even know you have them.* / It's not your fault. Having bed bugs in your home has nothing to do with its cleanliness. Cockroaches, however . . . (see page 37).

BED BUGS ON MY MIND

By Brooke Borel, journalist and author of Infested: How the Bed Bug Infiltrated Our Bedrooms and Took Over the World

---

It's hard to sleep when you've got visions of bloodsuckers crawling on your sheets.

One month of insomnia had turned into two. Most mornings, I'd crawl out of bed covered in itchy red welts. At first I thought, ticks. As more appeared, maybe spiders. I contracted a skin infection from mindless scratching. One bite swelled so big it looked like my calf was birthing a baseball.

Eventually, my mysterious plague had a name: bed bugs.

And I'd thought it was just a childhood myth, as imaginary as the tooth fairy. Nope: Turns out, "Don't let the bed bugs bite" is really good advice.

I ripped off my bedding and emptied my drawers and spent hours vacuuming every crack in my rental apartment's parquet floors.

The size of a lentil, bed bugs are supposedly visible but also sneaky. I'd never *seen* them. But they were there, hiding in my home, infesting my thoughts.

I stood, frantic, in the fluorescent-lit basement of my building, stuffing armfuls of my life into a coin-operated washing machine. And then a dark speck on the mattress pad caught my eye. Lint? I brought the gauzy white fabric closer. And there we were, assailant and victim, eye to eye.

Like I said, I was sleep deprived. I blame my bad bed-bug manners on that. But truth is, I panicked: I flicked that vermin as hard as I could. Where it landed, I don't know.

Possibly on that neatly folded pile of laundry in the corner?

Neighbors, forgive me.

BEES, WASPS, AND HORNETS

/ *Also known as: Stingers.*

FOUND Ruining summer picnics across the country.

SIZE As big as a paper clip.

It's a rite of passage: first time, first speeding ticket, first Shake Shack burger, first bee sting. It'll happen eventually (not necessarily in that order). And it's happening more and more, especially in Alaska, says allergist-immunologist Dr. Jeffrey Demain. Reports of people seeking care for "stinging events" are up 48 percent.

Bees, wasps, hornets . . . ideally, we'd just let them be. But alas, there's watermelon to eat and lawns to mow and weeds to whack, which is when most encounters occur, says Demain: "You go to trim a shrub and accidentally upset a four-foot wasp's nest."

About 4 percent of Americans are sensitive to insect stings. Signs are sweating, swelling, and passing out. Scarier: About sixty people a year die from stings. No need to be one of them.

WHAT TO DO

Don't entice: no perfume, no cologne (please). But yes to deodorant, body odor attracts bees; sweat actually angers them. That "no floral prints" thing? It's BS, says Demain.

When a bee starts bugging you, don't swat. It'll just piss it off. Stand as still as a statue. Step on a log and you are suddenly swarmed? *Run.* You're just as fast as a bee, but it'll usually give up before you do. Jumping in a lake won't save you: they'll just wait until you resurface.

Get the stinger out ASAP, before the venom spreads. Don't pinch—it'll sink further. Flick it off with your fingernail or a credit card. Wasps, yellow jackets, and hornets don't leave a stinger— *they just keep going.* Ouch.

Wash with soap and apply ice. If you start breaking out in hives or gasping— bust out the EpiPen or call 911.

But typically, a sting or two isn't cause for alarm. A laugh? Perhaps. Just google "bee-stung lips Jose," as 12 million people have, to see what two wasps can do to one man searching for his car keys.

MOST PAINFUL PLACE TO GET STUNG?
Your tongue, says Justin Schmidt, author of *The Sting of the Wild*, who's been stung at least 1,000 times. *Everywhere*. Close second? Inside your nose. (Unclear how that happens.)

BISON

/ *Also known as: American buffaloes, although historians hate when people call them that.*

FOUND Roaming the Great Plains, particularly Yellowstone National Park, since prehistoric times.

SIZE Up to 2,000 pounds; heaviest land mammal in North America (so don't mess with them).

SOUNDS High-pitched bleats, deep rumbles, low grunts.

A hundred years ago, bison were on the brink of extinction. Nineteenth-century settlers had massacred 50 million of them for food, for fun, and to infuriate the Native Americans, who considered them sacred. (That devastating hunt scene in *Dances with Wolves*? Bison.) Today there are only 30,000 or so wild bison in North America and about 400,000 livestock.

Organic bison burgers with smoked Gouda on a brioche bun are all the rage. Poor bison etiquette is too. For some reason, people think they can pet bison or take selfies with them or cuddle a baby because it looks cold. Fact: Bison are fat, furry, well-insulated animals; they don't get cold. They can get spooked though. If provoked, get the hell out of their way. And pray.

WHAT TO DO

If a bison is blocking a Yellowstone road, yield. Slow down, be patient, and wait for it to move—no honking, no speeding away; just chill and enjoy the scenery. It's rare, but bison have been known to attack cars—and anyone who stupidly gets out of their car. Hiking or biking when a bison gets in your way? Give it a wide berth, a football field's worth. Especially during rutting season, July through August: Mama bison are mean. If you see one paw the ground or shake its head or snort or raise its tail or, god forbid, charge—at 40 mph—with its two-foot-long horns coming straight at you . . . good luck.

GORED BY SELFIE

Five people were injured by bison in Yellowstone in 2015. They were three to six feet from the bison. The minimum distance you should be from a bison, per park rules, is seventy-five feet.

BLACK WIDOW SPIDERS

/ *Also known as: The female arachnids that eat the guys after sex*

FOUND In woodpiles, basements, and garages around North America.

SIZE A quarter, with legs.

SOUNDS The spider itself is silent. The sound of its messy web breaking, by human touch, is crinkly, crackling, and eerie.

No need to panic, but black widows seem to be hiding out lately in bunches of grapes. Not long ago, a Michigan woman reached into a bag she bought at Walmart and screamed. So did a BJ's Wholesale Club shopper in Pennsylvania . . . Boston . . . Wisconsin. . . . Black widows have been found hitching rides on store-bought fruit into homes around the country. Growers don't spray insecticides as much as they used to, which is good news for our food but bad news for arachnophobes and for anyone who accidentally gets bitten.

Despite their pretty red hourglass figure, female black widows are the most venomous spiders in North America. They rarely sink their fangs into humans. (Just don't sit on one.)

But if you do feel the pinprick of a black widow—and it is just a prick, the real pain comes later—expect swelling, followed by sweating, sharp pains like a punch in the stomach, a paralysis of the diaphragm that causes shortness of breath . . . oh, and puking. You probably won't die, though. Despite 2,500 black widow run-ins reported annually in the United States, it appears only one or two people ever have, says Dr. Paula Cushing, an evolutionary biologist who studies arachnids at the Denver Museum of Nature & Science. Rick Vetter, an entomologist at the University of California, Riverside, agrees. "Poison control says six or seven deaths due to spiders a year, but their numbers are always suspect. People don't die from black widow bites, not anymore."

WHAT TO DO

Remain calm and call poison control, stat. Jumping around will only speed the spread of the spider's venom in your bloodstream. Please don't try and suck it out like you're Michael Clarke Duncan in *The Green Mile*. (Do you really think that works?) Wash the site with soapy water. Apply ice and await the arrival of the antivenom. (Or the Ativan.)

FEAR FACTOR
Female black widows are
the most poisonous spider in
North America. Their venom
is fifteen times more powerful
than a rattlesnake's.

BOBCATS

/ *Also known as: Wildcats; named after their tail, which is stubby— that is, bobbed.*

FOUND Prowling forests, swamps, deserts, and suburbs in forty-eight states; most common wildcat in the country.

SIZE About twice as big as the average tabby.

SOUNDS They rarely vocalize, but when they do, they hiss, yowl, and wail like a crying kid.

Recurring theme in this book: Don't feed wildlife. Predators follow prey, as they say. And bobcats are certainly predators. They silently stalk and then pounce, going for the jugular. They love rabbits, rodents, feral cats, and birds. Anything already dead will do, too. If the opportunity arises, they'll go after guys bigger than them (like a deer), no problem. They are elusive and shy and *really* not into people.

People are into them, though, or at least into their pretty speckled fur. Humans have historically been bobcats' biggest killers, and lately it seems we're getting back into it. Illinois held its first bobcat hunt in four decades last year.

So feel bad for the bobcat! Don't be afraid. Though if you're, say, taking out the trash and suddenly a big kitty appears—okay, well, yeah.

WHAT TO DO

It'll typically dart before you can even identify it, but if it doesn't, and it starts growling? Something's wrong—it's probably rabid. So get the hell out of its way, grab your pets, and call Fish and Wildlife. Or you can try doing what one guy from Florida did when he got jumped: he got a good hold on its neck and choked it to death.

The bobcat population in the United States (2 to 3.7 million) has doubled since the 1990s in pretty much every state, thanks to protections and the fact that bobcats are so damn adaptable. / In the 1990s, there were 65 bobcat sightings reported in Connecticut. In 2015, there were 200.

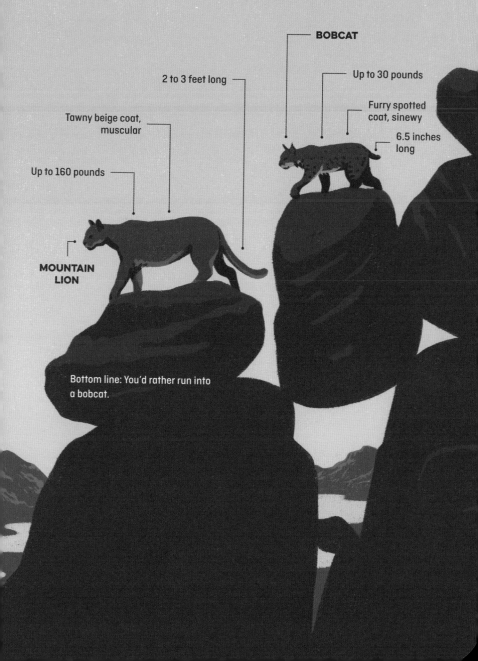

"No, that wasn't a mountain lion; it was a bobcat."
—Rangers to hikers, all the time

BOBCAT

Up to 30 pounds

2 to 3 feet long

Furry spotted coat, sinewy

Tawny beige coat, muscular

6.5 inches long

Up to 160 pounds

MOUNTAIN LION

Bottom line: You'd rather run into a bobcat.

COCKROACHES

/ *Also known as: Roaches,*
las cucarachas.

FOUND Crawling in kitchens, dorms, and dark, moist corners everywhere.

SIZE A thumbnail, hopefully no bigger.

SOUNDS Clicking.

In fifty years spent dealing with roaches, Cincinnati pest pro Rick Steinau has seen everything, including a living room wall covered with so many cockroaches, "it looked," he says, "like moving wallpaper."

Feel free to pretend otherwise, but there is a direct correlation between cleanliness and cockroaches. If you don't wash your dishes or empty your trash or mop your floor—cockroaches will come. The dirtier your home, the bigger your infestation, guaranteed, says Steinau.

Food is *all* they're after, and it comes in various forms: grilled cheese crumbs, cooking grease, that invisible glue that holds cardboard boxes together. You could sleep with a can of Raid (people do), but the real key is to let the roaches starve. And know this: if you see them during the day, you've got a real issue.

WHAT TO DO

Take away their snacks. Toss stacks of old magazines and stashes of paper bags. Don't leave food out, fruit bowls included. Rinse bottles and jars before recycling. Don't just wipe countertops and ovens; clean behind them.

What's the first step when you catch a cockroach crew coming through? Ideally, vacuum with a heavy-duty Dustbuster, though even a broom will do. Then dump everything into a Hefty bag. Before you cinch it tight and take it far, far away, sprinkle baby powder inside. Roaches' waxy shells are not unlike a baby's shiny bum; the powder sticks but will smother instead of soothe. Sprinkle an almost invisible layer on your floor, too.

Roach baits are good, says Steinau. Flushing agents are bad. "They just lure the roaches out of hiding; they start running—and then you've got a bigger problem."

If they persist, clear out your cabinets and closets, fob off your pet, and pony up the hundred bucks or so for a pro. Fingers crossed that'll do it on the first try or the second or. . . .

COCKROACHES IN NEW YORK (OF COURSE)

By Bonnie Tsui, journalist and author of American Chinatown

This is a classic New York tale: We were living in the city after college. My boyfriend, Matt, shared a two-bedroom walk-up with five roommates, including, more often than not, me. We slept in an alcove off the living room, separated by drywall and decorated with nothing but a desk and a futon mattress on the floor.

Soon enough, more roommates made themselves known. Mice chittered through bags of chips. Cockroaches skittered under the couch, in the kitchen, down the hallway.

I wished our mattress was not on the floor.

One day, one of Matt's human roommates went out and bought— not a mousetrap or a roach motel—but the Lexus of pest-eradication stations: The Rat Zapper 2000, a $40, battery-operated contraption that promised to take care of everything.

They set the Zapper down in a grungy corner of the kitchen, baited with cheese. And then they promptly forgot to look inside for oh, I don't know, weeks.

Finally, someone did look inside—not me—but I still throw up in my mouth a little bit to recall what was found: a dead mouse . . . being eaten by a swarm of cockroaches. The roaches were alive. Inside the Rat Zapper. Munching a mouse. THE ROACHES WERE ALIVE INSIDE THE RAT ZAPPER, MUNCHING A MOUSE. It was like the Turducken of household vermin.

Cringe. Collect yourself. Then marvel. The cockroach has essentially been around for 320 million years. It has persisted because it is able to survive tough times (decapitation, say, or starvation). But also because of its ability to eat anything: glue, fingernail clippings, each other. Mice.

RECIPE FOR ROACH-KILLER BALLS

2 tablespoons shortening
2 tablespoons sugar
1 cup Borax
½ cup all-purpose flour

Combine all the ingredients in a bowl, then slowly add enough water to make a soft dough. Roll the dough into balls, each about the size of an olive. Come nighttime, stash the balls where the roaches live. Replace as needed.

COWS

/ *Also known as: Cattle,*
heifers, bovines.

FOUND Grazing in pastures everywhere.

SIZE A little lighter than a Smart car.

SOUNDS Mooooooooo. . . .

There are roughly 92 million head of cattle in this country. A ratio of one cow to every three-and-a-half humans would be worrisome if cows were predators, but they're not. They're technically prey and typically innocuous, unless you're one of the million dairy farmers or ranchers in the United States who could be kicked or trampled or charged on any given workday. "We worry about older folks especially," says Dr. Wayne Sanderson, who researches agriculture safety at the University of Kentucky. "Farmers don't like to retire. They get old and slow and fat; have trouble seeing, hearing; and they don't realize the risk."

Be careful walking your dog through public farmland, too: between 1993 and 2013, fifty-four people were injured by cows in the UK countryside; one-quarter of them died.

WHAT TO DO

Give 'em six feet at least. Cows have personal space issues, too. They don't like it when people get too close. Also avoid stepping behind their butt. It's a blind spot.

If you come across a cow, just keep walking. Don't stop and stare (so rude). Keep your voice down (loud talkers agitate). Just let the cow chill, like it likes to: neck down, chewing its cud. But if it raises its head—get out of there. "Cows'll just come at ya without warning," says Sanderson.

Number-one rule: don't try and save your dog. Sorry.

DEATH BY HAMBURGER
Between 2003 and 2012, *E. coli*–tainted beef sickened 1,144 people, hospitalized 316, and killed 5. (Yum.)

HOW DO KILLER COWS STACK UP?
Sharks kill one American a year (see page 114). Snakes kill six Americans a year (see page 108). Cows kill twenty Americans a year.

BEWARE OF BULLS . . .

You'll find them on farms, ranches, and . . . New York City streets? A wise bull or three has been known to bust out of the slaughterhouse and barrel through Queens (in which case, Jon Stewart invites it home to his wife's animal sanctuary upstate). The last three decades have seen 261 bull attacks; 149 were fatal. Bulls are bigger and meaner than cows. Keep your distance. Never turn your back. And if the bull gets aggressive—head lowered, shoulders raised, snorting, pawing, staring you down—*run for your life*. "A charging bull will head-butt, knock ya down, and start stompin'," says Sanderson. Not pretty.

BY THE NUMBERS
Only two people have been killed by coyotes
in North America, including a folksinger in Nova
Scotia in 2009. National Geographic made
a short film about it, called . . . *Killed by Coyotes*.

COYOTES

/ *Also known as: "Barking dogs."*
(Makes sense.)

FOUND Slinking through fields, forests, mountains—and increasingly, cities.

SIZE A typical toddler.

SOUNDS Barks, yips, growls, howls.

Coyotes used to roam plains in the Midwest. Now they're chillin' on rooftops in Queens, running alongside cars in San Francisco, even raising pups in parking lots in Chicago. Ranchers hate them for killing their lambs, dog owners hate them for preying upon their poodles, and joggers worry they'll be chased down and chomped.

The Humane Society claims that more people are killed by flying champagne corks than by coyotes. Perhaps? But, what *is* known: coyote bites are up. America's coyote population is "likely" at an all-time high, experts say. That's a good thing given that one coyote eats 1,500 rodents a year. It's a not-so-good thing when you hear about coyotes biting, say, eleven people last year, in Southern California alone (up from four in 2014 and one in 2013), according to the California Department of Fish and Wildlife.

They're opportunistic omnivores, but they don't eat people. They will gorge on rabbits, rats, and rubbish, though. They really love fruit, says Camilla Fox, founder and executive director of Project Coyote. Coyotes have no qualms climbing an apple tree. But please don't feed them. "A fed coyote is a dead coyote," she says—the less afraid they are of us, the more aggressive they will get.

WHAT TO DO

If a coyote starts trailing you and your dog, it's just curious. Keep calm. Channel your inner frat guy and "haze" it, says Fox—no beer funnels, only bold actions. "Be big, bad, and loud."

Hiding behind a bush won't help alter coyote behavior in the long term. Yelling will. Stand tall, make eye contact, wave your arms, and bark "Go away!" Bang pots, blow a bullhorn. (You know you want one.)

Don't haze a mom with pups. Just look big and slink away. Otherwise throw rocks, scoop up pets and babies—and definitely don't start sprinting. Wile E. Coyote may never have caught Road Runner, but a real coyote could certainly catch you.

COYOTES IN MY FACE

By Chris Colin, journalist and coauthor of What to Talk About

———————————

I was young and moronic, bleary in the early morning, twitchy at each crunching twig. I'd never camped alone, let alone without a tent. Among the dry grass and gnarled oaks, I spent four days fixated on mountain lions, and the certainty I'd be dragged from my sleeping bag by the scalp. Now something was rustling to my left.

Clutching the walking stick I'd whittled to a nonlethal point, I braced for death, only to discover . . . turkeys. Strutting mindlessly through some manzanitas. I laughed out loud. Then turned back around—to a coyote, his long snout not two feet from mine.

The only coyote I'd ever seen was in cartoon form. This one was rather real. A sweet-looking beast with a bushy tail and an obvious curiosity, about me.

Later I'd struggle to explain how I could've been terrified of non-existent cougars yet totally unfazed by a coyote more or less in my lap. Truth is, something was *going on* between us. For a full minute, we stared into each other's eyes, two creatures communing peacefully and improbably across the vast chasm that separates us.

Then, as humans do, I ruined the moment. I reached for my goddamn camera.

I'll never forget the look of betrayal that flashed over the coyote's face as my shutter clicked. He actually cocked his head, baffled by my lameness. Our spell broken, it gave me one last glance, then trotted off on its elegant toothpick legs and vanished into the trees.

The photo? Haven't looked at it since.

CROWS

/ Also known as: Nature's cleanup crew, world's smartest birds.

FOUND Formerly in rural areas, increasingly in suburbs, cities, and circling above garbage bins everywhere.

SIZE Twice as big as a blue jay.

Used to be, only farmers cared about crows—getting into their crops, attacking their calves. A decent-looking scarecrow would do the trick. Crows were reticent, respectful, and by the early 2000s, decimated by West Nile virus. But now the black-feathered scavengers are back, big-time.

"They're moving into suburbs and cities because we're making it easy for them," says John Marzluff, professor of wildlife science at The University of Washington and author of *In the Company of Crows.* We're providing Dumpsters of food, tall trees for roosting, and leafy parks with picnic areas.

Crow populations are rising exponentially, he says. In Seattle, there are thirty to forty times more crows than there were in the 1960s. In the 1980s, the Golden Gate Audubon Oakland Christmas crow count hovered between 30 and 90 crows. In 2010, it was 1,100. Aspen has lots of crows now, when thirty years ago, it didn't.

More people, more crows, means more people-crow contact. And the more they see us, the less they fear us, says Marzluff. Indeed, from Queens to Queensland, reports of crow attacks have been pouring in. A site called CrowTrax has crowd-sourced thousands of crow attacks around Vancouver. And it's kind of addictive:

REAL-LIFE ENTRIES

"Was standing, no problem, started to attack me after I lit a cigarette, recognizes me now whenever I walk this block. Aggressiveness: 4."

"A crow pecked at my friend's head and there was blood. Aggressiveness: 5."

"I was dive-bombed by two in tandem a total of six times. Aggressiveness: 5."

"Crow going through recycling and making a mess, yelled at it and it started to attack. Aggressiveness: 2."

Prime time is spring and summer, when parents are protective of their new young. Crows are like humans, says Marzluff: intelligent, loud, family-oriented, and big fans of KFC.

They also tend to stick together for their own safety. A murder (yes, that's what it's called) of 2 million crows was once found roosting in Fort Cobb, Oklahoma. (Who's gonna mess with that?)

The craziest thing: crows remember faces, *for years*. So don't piss them off. A man in Seattle once picked up a dead crow in his backyard and was dubbed a crow-killer. Harassed by the birds for months, he eventually moved . . . in the middle of the night. Another crow target grew a goatee and a moustache, let his hair get longer, donned different hats, and still, the crow was not fooled.

Know that if you feed a crow it'll come back for more . . . and bring friends. Steer clear unless you want a crow companion; some people do. There's a librarian in Washington who made sausage and eggs every morning for ten years for a bird named Bella. Otherwise, it's best to never initiate contact. And try not to walk by a nest; the crows may go crazy.

CONTINUED

WHAT TO DO

Face the crow head-on. They prefer to attack from behind. Cross the street. Carry an umbrella. Don't throw rocks, or they'll literally come back to bite you—routinely. If things get bad, you could try a disguise. "But it'd have to be a good disguise," says Marzluff.

Wearing a surgeon's mask has been helpful, but not foolproof. It's also not a bad idea to carry unshelled peanuts to scatter on the ground. But even feeding it might not help, says Marzluff. If the crow really hates you, you're pretty much screwed.

Crows can be picky. An experiment showed crows prefer french fries in a McDonald's bag over those in a plain brown paper bag. / The oldest crow in captivity lived to be fifty-nine years old. / Australian magpies are worse, says Marzluff. "They'll actually poke your eyes out."

DEER

/ *Also known as: Fawns, bucks, does.*

FOUND In forests, fields, and leafy suburbs.

SIZE A little shorter than the average Olympic gymnast and just as lean.

Wildlife biologists debate whether deer populations are still on the rise, but whether we've got 31 million or 34 million deer in the United States, it's still a lot of deer, 100 times more than there were 100 ago.

More deer means (1) more ticks (see page 126) and (2) more car crashes—1.25 million a year. According to State Farm's annual claims report, more drivers are hitting deer than ever. Statistically, white-tailed deer kill more people a year (about 200) than any other animal in North America. It's funny that deer aren't as feared as bears and mountain lions—they should be.

Rick Kamura of Russ's Body & Paint Shop in Missoula, Montana, has been dealing with deer accidents for thirty-seven years, but lately, he says, it's gotten worse. In the fall, he'll get at least four deer collision calls a week. (Or moose, elk, bighorns.) Once a fish was at fault. It fell out of an eagle's mouth and onto the interstate. Gills and guts all over the windshield. "We meet by accident," says Kamura. "That's our slogan."

WHAT TO DO

Keep your eyes peeled while driving, especially at dawn and dusk. Stop texting behind the wheel. Seatbelts and working headlights are key. And know if you see one deer leaping, there are more on its heels.

Ideally, you hit the brakes before hitting the deer. If not, keep driving. Don't swerve. Colliding with a car barreling toward you at 50 mph is worse than running into a buck. Plus, cars can be replaced—you can't.

ATTACK OF THE BAMBIS

Very occasionally, deer get aggressive. The leafy town of Ashland, Oregon, has had a real issue in recent years: people walking their dogs have been knocked down and cut up by hooves. "If a deer's pinning its ears and stomping, get outta there," says Mark Vargas of the Oregon Department of Fish and Wildlife. If it comes at you, antlers and all: Fight back. Get behind a tree. And please, "Stop feeding deer," begs Vargas. "That's how we got into this problem in the first place."

DEER IN THE SUBURBS

By Vanessa Hua, author of Deceit and
Other Possibilities

Where I grew up in the oak-studded hills, hitting a deer was a rite of passage. At night, the roads were dark and winding, and we always drove too fast, trying to make curfew. We felt invincible, glorious. Right up until someone rammed into a buck, made just as bold from a lack of apex predators in the burbs. Our eyes locked with his, caught in the proverbial headlights in that eternal moment before impact.

And then it was decision time: call animal control—or lug it to our teacher.

Alive, deer are beguiling, the flick of their tails, their graceful tiptoeing. If I startled the deer, their hooves against the sidewalk sounded like stiletto heels.

Dead, deer got us extra credit. My high school biology teacher was a connoisseur of fresh roadkill, with a coonskin cap he'd stitched together like Davy Crockett and a freezer in his garage packed with self-butchered bargains.

One morning, our class watched, fascinated and disgusted, as he dissected a pregnant doe. Her eyes had gone glassy, but her body was not yet stiff. With a scalpel, he sliced open her belly to reveal a cloudy amniotic sac. Then the smell hit, insides suddenly on the outside.

We recoiled but could not tear ourselves from what we saw next: a glistening, perfect pair of fawns who looked like they were sleeping, as if they might suddenly open their eyes and prance onto our lawns and into the cul-de-sacs we all called home. It was a lesson my teacher somehow knew was impossible for a bunch of teenagers to find in any textbook: death reminding us of the wonders of life.

DOGS

/ *Also known as: Mutts,*
bitches, man's best friend.

FOUND In backyards, parks, and laps everywhere.

SIZE Small as a baby, big as a pony.

"Like it or not, American dog owner, your pet is a hazard," journalist Farhad Manjoo wrote in a brilliant piece entitled "No, I Do Not Want to Pet Your Dog." Oh, he probably wasn't talking about *your* cute dog; he meant your neighbor's dog or that rottweiler running at you off-leash; or the mean-looking dogs sprawled along San Francisco's Haight Street. He was talking about feral dogs, for sure.

Apologies to dog people everywhere, as this is not easy to hear, but: dogs, all kinds of dogs, bite 4.7 million people a year; one in five bites becomes infected with bad stuff like rabies or tetanus; and twenty to thirty people die, annually, at the paws of someone who is supposed to be your best friend.

That's more people than sharks, alligators, snakes, and bears kill combined. And yet people love pups anyway! About 40 percent of American households have one. Adorable, sweet dogs, until, one day, they're not.

WHAT TO DO

The obvious: always get the okay from the dog before going in for a pet. Tugging tails: never smart. If a stranger or stray comes sniffing (and you're not, like, a diehard dog lover) be "still like a tree," advises the Centers for Disease Control and Prevention. Avoid eye contact or smiling. Stand to its side. Sternly say, "Go home." No squirming—they'll sense your nervousness. And definitely don't run. Total trigger.

Wait for the dog to move on. If it starts growling, slowly cover your neck with your hands. If it goes for you and its teeth sink in, don't fight. Put a bag or coat between the two of you. Otherwise, curl into a ball, wait for it to be over, and admit you might be more of a cat person.

More than 50 percent of dog bites occur on your own property. / Kids ages five to nine get bitten the most. / Between 2005 and 2016, 392 Americans were killed by dogs. / Pit bull advocates will balk, but according to dogbite.org, pits were responsible for 65 percent of these deaths; rottweilers, 11 percent.

DONKEYS

/ *Also known as: Burros,
jacks, jennies, asses.*

FOUND Mostly in Africa and China, but 0.1 percent of the world's 41 million-strong donkey population resides in North America.

SIZE Up to 1,100 pounds, but those adorable mini-donkeys Reese Witherspoon used to have are equivalent to your carry-on.

SOUNDS Braying—a real hee-haw or "eeyore" (as in *the* Eeyore).

There are horse people and cat people and the aforementioned dog people. There are also donkey people, more than you might think. They even have their own magazine: *Mules and More.*

"I'd wager people with pet donkeys is at its highest since the late 1800s," says Steve Stiert, who teaches Donkeys 101 at the State University of New York Ulster and leads a donkey meetup group in the Hudson Valley. Membership is nearing 600.

In Oatman, Arizona, carrot-toting tourists feed the wild burros. In Colorado, people run with donkeys. It's called pack burro racing, and with a slogan like "Celebrating 70 Years of Hauling Ass," what's not to love? Occasionally, elsewhere in the United States, donkeys are hired to carry backpackers' gear or guard farmers' pigs or mow homeowners' lawns.

And very occasionally, these docile, overgrown dogs—who like a good rub between the ears and will be your lifelong buddy—attack.

"They're highly territorial," says Jan Dohner, author of *Livestock Guardians.* And when threatened, they'll charge, strike with their hooves, and bite your butt with their big-ass donkey teeth.

Donkeys eat: mostly grass, about 6,000 pounds per year. / Donkeys live: for about thirty years. (Oldest recorded donkey was fifty-four, Suzy from New Mexico.) / Donkeys kill: mostly small dogs, not humans. Though, not long ago, a 500-pound donkey did trample to death the mayor of a small town in Texas.

WHAT TO DO

"Well, there's not much you *can* do, except get away," says Dohner. To avoid getting into a dangerous donkey situation in the first place, geld your donkey. "Intact males are less predictable than stallions," says Dohner. Read its signals: ears back, tail swishing, head swinging—not good.

"Never turn your back on a jack" is a good motto. Don't corner it either, or enter the enclosure of a donkey you don't know. And definitely, steer clear of its rear.

DUST MITES

/ *Also known as: Mites.*

FOUND Tucked into beds in 84 percent of U.S. homes, especially in the summertime.

SIZE Too microscopic to see, thankfully, or you'd have serious insomnia.

Attention 20 million Americans allergic to dust mites: you're sleeping with the enemy—millions of them, every night. These tiny translucent bugs that feed on flakes of human skin and drop invisible feces between your sheets, all over your blankets, and inside your pillows, leave you feeling, in the morning, like the star of a 1980s Nyquil commercial: sniffling, sneezing, aching, coughing, stuffy head . . . wheezing, with itchy red watery eyes and a runny nose you can't stop rubbing. It's a good look.

WHAT TO DO

Dust, for starters. Just wear a mask while you do, or your allergies will get even worse. Dust mites can't stand high heat or freezing cold, so move to Sedona or Alaska—or, some say: cram your pillow or kids' stuffed animals or favorite shirt in the freezer for a couple of hours.

Wash your bedding weekly at a minimum of 130°F. Flood your bedroom with sunlight. Declutter. Vacuum everything, all the time: curtains, mattresses, carpets (or better idea: hardwood). Air it all outside once in a while, and cover in allergen-proof casings, advises the American Academy of Allergy, Asthma & Immunology.

Ditch all of your wool sweaters, unfortunately. (Wool is a dust mite's favorite food—after the skin you shed.) A dehumidifier is a good idea, too, as dust mites multiply in humidity.

Keep things light and airy, the opposite of clammy. Which, you realize, means you should leave your bed *unmade* every morning. (Sorry, Mom.)

Female dust mites lay one to three eggs a day. / One dust mite can produce twenty droppings a day. / A dust mite's life span is six to eight weeks. / The number of dust mites on your mattress is anywhere from 100,000 to 10,000,000. (Good night.)

DIY DUST MITE DETERRENT

In a spray bottle, add 2 teaspoons each of eucalyptus and peppermint essential oils and 2 cups of water. Shake to combine. Spray bedding, clothes, and carpets—often.

ELEPHANT SEALS

/ *Also known as: Sea elephants, bulls.*

FOUND Lolling along the California coast, down to Baja, up to Oregon, with a few stragglers as far north as Washington.

SIZE Big-rig big, up to twenty feet long and 8,800 pounds.

SOUNDS Snorts and grunts, like a long and epic burp.

And the award for World's Ugliest Mammal goes to . . . the elephant seal. Once hunted to near extinction and later protected, elephant seals are now recolonizing sites along the California coast where they used to be. Populations are rising roughly 6 percent a year. The latest estimate is 239,000 and counting.

Most of their lives are spent underwater, trying to avoid orcas—but once or twice a year, these prehistoric creatures slither onto the mainland, where they lie around, living off their blubber, doing nothing but dozing, fighting, fornicating, and birthing.

At Año Nuevo State Park, tourists and school groups pile in daily for guided walks, weaving safely through the sand among thousands of molting mounds. But increasingly, elephant seals are colonizing less-controlled areas like Piedras Blancas, where a 4,000-pound seal recently barreled through a fence onto the boardwalk.

According to local rangers' lore, a dad once plopped his daughter on top of an elephant seal to snap a picture. It reared up, tossed the girl, and bit the father's leg, leaving a gaping hole. "Stuff like this is happening more and more," says interpreter Mike Merritt. "People see a seal and have no idea."

WHAT TO DO

Whisper. Never get between two seals. And please keep your distance—a minimum of 25 feet, says Merritt. The National Marine Fisheries Service recommends 300 feet. Luckily, these massive animals have zero interest in humans. You're lucky if they even wake up when you walk by.

If one ever appears to be coming after you, it's only because a bigger bull is chasing it. An elephant seal is faster than it looks. "It's like a runaway truck," warns Merritt, "you just gotta get out of its way."

A male seal can impregnate up to fifty ladies in one season. / Their teeth are as long as your fingers but fortunately dullish. / Still, when an elephant seal *does* bite someone, it's usually a scientist. And it's usually in the butt.

FOXES

/ *Also known as: Sly and shy.*

FOUND Slinking around forests and farms and, unfortunately, in chicken coops coast to coast.

SIZE As big as a border collie.

SOUNDS You rarely hear one, but keep your ears open for a yip or screamy howl.

It used to be big news when you saw a fox, because they were so seldom seen. Red, gray, arctic, and kit foxes—lately they seem to be everywhere: Kansas City; New York City; famously, Facebook headquarters; and apparently, all over London.

And for some reason, urbanites and suburbanites don't seem to be freaking out. Mark Zuckerberg was so happy about his new family of foxes, he had Facebook's Menlo Park campus certified as an official wildlife habitat. The company even started selling stuffed animal foxes in blue Facebook tees.

Still, not *everyone* wants a den of foxes—and their newly born kits—dwelling under their deck.

WHAT TO DO

Encourage the foxes to move out. Harass them like a landlord trying to oust long-term renters paying below-market rates. Cram their doorways with leaves or smelly old sneakers and socks. Bang pots. Leave a transistor radio on overnight. Install an automatic sprinkler that goes off, say, every morning at 4 a.m. Fox parents are like people parents; they just want to give their kids a nice, safe place to live.

If you see a lone fox in the park or in your backyard, it'll likely flee before you can yell "Go away!" If it doesn't budge, throw a tennis ball, spray a hose. And if it's staggering around like some drunk dude or starts coming at you at 30 mph (which would be really rare), it's likely rabid.

Foxes mate for life, which is impressive. Then again, they live for only about three years. / A single red fox can wipe out an entire coop in one midnight raid. Winner, winner, chicken dinner.

FRUIT FLIES

/ *Also known as: Gnats.*

FOUND Flitting around your kitchen.

SIZE Somewhere between an ant and a housefly.

It looks so good on the counter: a fruit bowl brimming with berries and cherries and peaches and plums, just plucked from the farmers' market. Wait a few warm summer days, though, and whatever has yet to be eaten . . . probably won't be. Because your once beautiful fruit bowl is now swarming with fruit flies. As is the compost bin.

Soon, your kitchen is overrun with fruit flies—little gnats that lay up to 500 eggs at a time, all over your overripe avocados, and then refuse to leave.

WHAT TO DO

Relinquish your fruit-bowl fantasies and refrigerate whatever you can. (Cold grapes taste better anyway.) Keep kitchen windows closed. Screens don't cut it; fruit flies are small enough to squeeze through. Keep a fan blowing. Mop with extra vengeance. Regularly wash out your trash can, recycling bin, and composter—and make sure to rinse applesauce jars before tossing.

To destroy fruit flies, you basically need to drown them. So concoct some sort of liquid trap. A bottle of unfiltered apple cider vinegar, say. Cover the top in plastic wrap, use a rubber band to hold it in place, and poke a bunch of holes with a toothpick, big enough for the fruit fly to fall in, but not fly out. A bottle of soda works, too, with a couple of holes hammered into the plastic lid. The only thing flies love more than Coke: wine. Roll a paper cone and invert it into an almost-empty bottle of red, add a splash of dish soap, a few pieces of rotten banana, and buh-bye. For now.

Fruit flies and humans share 75 percent of disease-causing genes, which is why researchers love them. And, in the name of science, we *should* too. / It's not just fruit. They'll breed anywhere stuff ferments: in garbage disposals, drains, dumpsters, mop buckets, and empty beer cans. (There's your extra motivation to clean up post party.)

GOOSE, THE VERB

To poke someone between the buttocks with an upward thrust. Merriam-Webster didn't just make that up. If a goose comes flying or running toward you—as they've been known to do, during nesting season, especially—duck, while somehow still looking it in the eye. Don't swing, it'll just get madder. And never turn your back on a goose. Or, you know, you might get goosed.

GEESE

/ *Also known as: Honkers.*

FOUND Flying the friendly skies and waddling around ponds, playgrounds, and people's manicured backyards across North America.

SIZE Bigger than a duck; smaller than a swan.

There are two kinds of Canada geese: Those that migrate (migratory) and occasionally fly into airplane engines, à la Sully's Miracle on the Hudson. And those that hunker down near humans (resident) and crap their brains out.

Once on the brink of extinction, there are now some 6 million geese in North America—the majority resident—the population of which has exploded since 1980 from 300,000 to approximately 4.5 million today, says Dr. Paul Curtis, wildlife specialist at Cornell University.

The problem is, one goose squeezes out two to three pounds of poop every day. It's disgusting, people say, a hindrance to walking barefoot in their own backyards! But it's also a public health hazard: feces carry *E. coli* and salmonella, capable of fouling water supplies and forcing temporary beach closures, says Curtis.

On public parks, soccer fields, and golf courses, the geese have gotten so bad that city officials in Washington DC and Boston have called in the pros.

Yes, goose poop removal is a profession. Geese Relief deploys specially trained border collies to chase the geese away, once a day. But companies like Scoopy Doo and DoodyCalls do the dirty work. (And they do dog poop, too.)

WHAT TO DO

Stop mowing. (No-mow lawns are more fashionable anyway.) Train your own border collie. Hardworking herding dogs, they won't actually eat the birds; they stare and sprint and intimidate them into nesting elsewhere. Try a floating alligator head. Available on Amazon! Plastic coyote effigies that spin on poles help too. A cute stuffed coyote might do the trick—if you move it around. Geese aren't stupid.

HORSES

/ Also known as: Mares, stallions, colts, fillies, Black Beauty, and a million other film and literary mounts.

FOUND On farms, ranches, and in sanctuaries—plus 55,000 roaming wild and free around the West.

SIZE One horse can weigh as much as a couple of Harleys.

"More people come into the emergency room for horse-related injuries than for motorcycle accidents," says Jason Hanley, an ER doctor in Washington. "And they look just as bad."

Thirty million people ride horses in America (it's unclear whether that includes pony rides, and petting zoos—ew). As beautiful as horses are, they're also kind of treacherous.

One in five riders is injured from a fall; one in three from just standing near a horse. Head injuries, busted torsos, broken bones, total paralysis like Christopher Reeve, too. And death, around twenty people every year.

Professional horse jockeys have it the worst: thirteen have died on the track since 2000. (Though the racehorses are the real victims: hundreds of horses die every year at racetracks across America.)

Still, regular horse people tend to treat their horses just fine, if not always safely.

WHAT TO DO

Odds are, a horse will gallop away when it gets spooked. (Hopefully not when you're on it.) Wear a helmet whether you're in the saddle or standing on the soil, a recent study concluded. Julie Goodnight, of DirectTV's *Horse Master*, outlines a horse's three weapons "in order of deadliness": teeth, front legs, back legs (i.e., biting, striking, kicking).

So stay in front or below its face and out of its blind spots. If you have to go behind a horse, place your hand on its body and keep talking, gently, like Bob Ross. Stay out of a horse's mouth. And if it starts "lipping" you—that's a prelude to a bite, not a kiss.

WILD, WILD HORSES

As controversial as they are, a bunch of mustangs in the middle of nowhere is still an amazing thing to witness. Adhere to the obvious if you encounter a wild herd: keep 100 feet away, don't feed them (they eat grass, thank you), and don't scream "This is so cool!!" and startle them. You really don't want to be caught in a stampede.

JAGUARS

/ *Also known as:* El tigre.

FOUND Mostly South and Central America and now . . . Arizona?

SIZE Massive, the third-largest cat in the world after lions and tigers.

SOUNDS A true roar, like a deep chesty cough.

A century or two ago, these extra-big cats ranged from Argentina all the way to California. And then, after near-extinction in the United States, a lone jaguar showed up in 2011, prowling around the Santa Rita Mountains outside of Tucson. A spotted, beautiful (and terrifying looking) young adult male, he was named "El Jefe"—aka "The Boss"— by a bunch of local middle school students who were thrilled to have him. Considering there are only 15,000 jaguars left in the world, it was quite a treat.

El Jefe likely slipped across the border from Mexico, where 80 to 120 jaguars still roam, as 7 have done since the 1990s. Only now, lucky for us, trail camera technology is catching them.

He stayed Stateside for a while but eventually must've gotten lonely, as the last recording of him was in 2015. Rumors are, he either went home to hunt for a mate, met his demise, or is avoiding the spotlight. He could've made new friends—two different jaguars have since been spotted in the mountains of southern Arizona, including one caught on camera in the Chiricahua Mountains by the Center for Biological Diversity. Say hello to Sombra (or maybe don't). According to Mark Hart of Arizona Game and Fish, there are likely more on the way.

WHAT TO DO

Only one person saw El Jefe in the flesh, a hunter who left him alone. Odds are good you'll never see a jaguar anywhere but the San Diego Zoo . . . hopefully. Its bite is so strong, it can crack a turtle like we do a hard-shell taco. If you do spot one while you're hiking sometime—or swimming (jaguars love the water)— react like it's a mountain lion, says Hart (see page 84).

MEET OCELOTS: MINI BIG-CATS

Bigger than Fluffy, smaller than El Jefe, the first ocelot kittens in two decades have been spotted in South Texas, a clan of cute, but not cuddly spotted cats. Still, with only about fifty left in the country, drive carefully.

JELLYFISH

/ Also known as: Sea wasps
(box jellies) and floating terrors
(Portuguese man-of-wars).

FOUND Ruining beach days around the world.

There are hundreds of jellyfish in the sea, but the ones to watch out for are those that can sting you. Or potentially kill you,* especially if you live in Australia or the Philippines or Thailand, home to the world's most lethal jellies.

Bad news for the 52 million Americans who swim in the ocean every year: 500,000 people are stung in the Chesapeake Bay alone; and 200,000 are stung off Florida. In New Hamsphire, one lion's mane jellyfish once washed up on shore and somehow its fragmented tentacles stung 150 people.

Still, the lion's mane jellyfish found in America "is a bit of a wuss," says Lisa Gershwin, a Tasmania-based jellyfish expert and author of *Stung!* It's the Portuguese man-of-war we need to worry about, which stings 500,000 people annually in the United States, sometimes fatally. It is "hands down" the deadliest in North America, warns Gershwin. And we're seeing more of them, as with many jellyfish, due to overfishing and warming seas.

It's unclear whether we're seeing more of the *Alatina moseri* genus of box jelly, the kind that contains the deadliest venom in the ocean, says Gershwin. But we know we don't want to. Not after watching what happened to Diana Nyad on her famed Cuba-to-Florida swim, when she was suddenly able to muster only one word from the water, albeit repeatedly: "Fire, fire, fire, fire, fire."

At Waikiki Beach, the Hawaiian *Alatina moseri* has been swarming inshore every month, ten days after the full moon. Its sting leads to Irukandji syndrome: intense pain, vomiting, cramping, sweating, difficulty breathing, and anxiety worse than Woody Allen's.

JELLYFISH FEAR?
There's an app for that. Lisa Gershwin's Jellyfish App Pro provides encyclopedic info, real-time alerts, and instant identification. Plus, a "Jellyfish Near Me" feature, to help avoid stings in the first place.

*Worldwide, jellyfish kill about fifty people a year. In the United States, though, it's "basically zero," says Dr. Lucas Brotz. "Thankfully we don't have the deadly species here like they do in the South Pacific, just species that pack a nasty sting."

WHAT TO DO

Understand what a purple flag in the sand means: stay out of the water. It makes for a bummer of a beach day, but it's better than thousands of toxic harpoons shooting into your leg. Slathering on anti-jelly lotion like Safe Sea can't hurt. "Stinger suits"—which create a barrier over your skin that the nematocysts can't penetrate—offer more protection, says Dr. Lucas Brotz, at the University of British Columbia's Institute for the Oceans and Fisheries.

If a jelly latches on, get it off—with tweezers or a stick, not your fingers. Douse the affected area with seawater. If it's a box jelly (found in Australia and the South Pacific, but also in Hawaii, Florida, North Carolina), try vinegar to neutralize the stinging cells. But—confusing—*don't* use vinegar on man-of-war or lion's mane stings, says Brotz. That'd make it *more* painful. What about urine? Nope. A study in Honolulu found that—contrary to popular belief— peeing on a jellyfish sting just makes it worse. Brotz suggests chatting up locals if you get stung, and doing what they do. Depending on the local species, sometimes cold packs help, sometimes hot packs help, and sometimes, *maaaybe* sprinkling McCormick's meat tenderizer on your leg like it's a lamb chop helps, too.

LICE

/ *Also known as: Head lice,
louse, the worst.*

FOUND On heads everywhere, mostly little ones.

SIZE A tad smaller than a sesame seed.

As long as there are children in this world, there will be lice in their hair, sucking blood from their scalps, and laying nits all over their locks. Lice drives parents to such desperation, we'll try anything to destroy them: slathering with mayonnaise, shampooing with beer, vinegar, or Vaseline. (None of this works, by the way, says Richard Pollack, a Harvard entomologist.)

We madly wash sheets, clothes, and stuffed animals. We pull our kids from school to spend all day scrubbing their heads with pesticide-based treatments and then painstakingly combing eggs out of every strand. Or we pay hundreds, sometimes thousands, of dollars to "salons," with names like Nit Picky and Licenders and LoveBugs, to do it for us.

Lice crawl from head to head, and multiply fast and furious—a single female will lay between 50 and 150 nits over her month-long life. Let it go unchecked for too long, and your tween will be topped with 2,000 eggs—like the worst case the San Francisco Hair Fairies has ever seen.

WHAT TO DO

Whatever your mom did when you had lice doesn't really seem to be working. (And, yes, it was always the moms . . . still is, actually, isn't it?) A lot of lice have grown resistant over the years to the ol' over-the-counter Rid or Nix routine. According to a recent study, 98 percent of head lice in the United States now carry gene mutations for pesticide resistance—up from 37 percent in 2001. So it's no surprise that new innovations have emerged.

The most promising, according to Pollack, is the FDA-registered AirAllé device used by Lice Clinics of America, a franchise proliferating (to five-star Yelp raves) almost as quickly as lice itself. The high-heat technology professes to kill lice and 92 percent of eggs in a single $150 visit—a relative bargain. But the cheapest, easiest guarantee? Shave your kid's head. Hair—it grows back.

HEAD CHECK
About one out of every hundred kids gets lice, Pollack estimates, typically between kindergarten and fourth grade. After that, it drops off. Thank god.

Mice don't just eat at night, by the way. They eat twenty times a day, all day. / A mouse can have a new litter of babies about every three weeks, which means, sorry: you've got more than one.

MICE

/ *Also known as: Mighty, Mickey, Stuart.*

FOUND In basements and cupboards, and under beds everywhere.

SIZE Like a butterball potato, plus that tail.

SOUNDS Squeak-squeak . . .

Mice and men have long been at odds. But Houston, you have a real problem. According to the American Housing Survey, 12 percent more households there reported having more rodents than two years ago (rats, too; see page 102). Being one of the fastest-growing cities in the country has its hazards. Among them: mice.

"Our phone's been ringing like crazy," says Chris Cooper of Texas-based Omega Animal Removal. "People with new multimillion-dollar homes call up perplexed: 'How can I have mice??' I'm like, Whaddaya think was there before your fancy development?"

A whopping 18 percent of households in Philadelphia report rodents; Boston is not far behind. Washington DC, Milwaukee, Cincinnati . . . mice-ridden cities all. Manhattan, of all places, saw a decline, but 1.1 million households with pests gnawing power cords and pooping in the pantry is plenty.

Mice. They're just like us! All they want is food, shelter, and warmth (i.e., check your toaster).

WHAT TO DO

"Has nothing to do with cleanliness," says Cooper, "just poor maintenance." Wonky gutters, worn garage doors, cracks in foundation: mouse house. Give them a gap as small as a dime, and they'll squeeze their way in.

To find the holes, sprinkle flour along a suspicious wall and then look for little footprints. You could spend a weekend plugging holes with copper mesh and quick-drying cement—or call the pros; preferably those who don't rely on poison. "If you seal everything up *and then* use poison, the mice will just die in the walls and stink up the place," warns Cooper.

Glue boards and electrocution gadgets are cruel. Grating a bar of Irish Spring soap supposedly deters them; they hate the minty smell. Otherwise, the classic snap trap remains the easiest—and most humane—way to ensnare. Hold the cheese, please, says Cooper. What mice really like is peanut butter.

MICE IN THE BACKSEAT

By Samin Nosrat, cook and author of Salt, Fat, Acid, Heat

———————————————

It was apricot season, and I wanted to make jam. I drove fifty miles to my favorite orchard, where the farmer loaded sixty pounds of absolutely perfect Blenheims into my Subaru. Then I drove fifty miles home.

Back in my kitchen, I saw pockmarks on the fruit, which was puzzling. I took a bite, and they were delicious nonetheless. I filled two dozen jars. A week later, lugging groceries out of the car, I noticed nibbles on my baguettes! And then I spotted her. And she spotted me. By the light of the streetlamp, we locked eyes, the mouse and me. Then she scampered under the seat— and out of reach.

I resolved to catch her.

The next day, I bought out the hardware store and baited traps with peanut butter. In the morning: no peanut butter, but no mouse either. I tried again and again.

Eventually, I sprinkled peppermint oil, thinking that'd coax her out. Nope, but my car smelled like candy cane for weeks.

It became like a bad bi-species buddy movie. Mouse as my copilot, munching my groceries, haunting my dreams. Until I realized, she liked what I had: food. I'd make her a smorgasbord! I'd invite her in for dinner, without letting her out.

So I took my tallest pot and prepared a buffet of crackers, cheese, cantaloupe, leftover pizza, and plenty of peanut butter. I put it behind the backseat so she could dive in, deep.

The next morning, there she was, still chowing down. As I carried the pot over to the compost bin, we looked at each other one last time before I dropped her in.

In Alaska, more people are injured by moose than by bear. / Moose eat seventy-three pounds of shrubs and grasses per day in summer, but as herbivores, they'll never eat you. / Some people eat moose, though; moose nose is a delicacy in some circles.

MOOSE

/ *Also known as: Really, really big deer.*

FOUND Up north, in colder climates like Alaska and Canada, Maine, Montana, the Rockies.

SIZE Taller than Shaquille O'Neal and five times as heavy.

It's Bullwinkle's fault—the bumbling, beloved 1960s cartoon has arguably made the moose a most misunderstood animal, for generations. Its gentle-giant, oafish look hasn't helped either, with a grand rack, knobby knees, oblong nose, and that furry wattle.

Though moose populations are in decline, people seem to be seeing more of them lately, in unlikely places: loitering outside martini lounges in Anchorage, galloping down sidewalks in suburban Boston, commandeering ski slopes in Steamboat, and giving birth in a Lowes parking lot.

In Canada, moose like to lick salt off cars while people are sitting in them. In Aspen, one charged a woman walking her dogs. Don't worry; she was okay. People attacked by moose usually are. Only one or two people die per year from moose encounters. There are plenty of fatal car accidents though; more moose die than humans, hundreds a year.

If one of these hulking creatures gets mad, especially bulls in fall rutting season and mamas in spring, *beware*. Moose are not predators. But they're also not afraid of much, people included. Plus, they've got knife-sharp hooves and powerful legs, and if they attack, it's because you've invaded their space. Says Mike Porras of Colorado Parks & Wildlife, "You face far more danger from a moose than you would a bear or a mountain lion." Marvelous.

WHAT TO DO

An Alaskan wildlife biologist once told a news reporter: "Assume every moose is a serial killer standing in the middle of the trail with a loaded gun."

Alrighty then: If you come across a moose close-up, back away slowly, palms up. If its ears pin back and its hackles raise and it starts smacking its lips—or peeing—expect a charge. Unlike bears, when it comes to moose, run like mad. Moose are just as fast, but they supposedly won't chase you very far. Plus, you are more nimble than a half-ton animal—get behind a boulder or tree. Or better yet, climb it. If you're attacked: now's the time to play dead.

MOSQUITOES

/ *Also known as: The deadliest creatures in the world. (Truth.)*

FOUND All summer long, especially at dawn and dusk.

SIZE Weighs less than a grain of sand.

SOUNDS A whining buzz in your ear when you're trying to sleep.

Female mosquitoes are out for blood—bird blood, horse blood, and as anyone who's been "eaten alive" knows, human blood. They especially like humans who are overheated and sweaty, heavy breathers, and have been drinking beer all day.

Not all 3,000 species transmit diseases, but the ones that do may kill a million people a year. In 2015, 429,000 people died from malaria alone. Worldwide, mosquitoes kill more people annually than people do.

In America, though, mosquitoes kill "only" 100 people per year—mostly from sporadic outbreaks of West Nile virus. The rest of us just get bitten up at barbecues, at the beach, in our sleeping bags—and hope that Zika doesn't continue to spread.

WHAT TO DO

Please, when it comes to mosquitoes, let's not get all PETA about it. They recommend popping B vitamins to avoid encounters in the first place, and it's worth a try. Try ditching your bird pond or koi pond or old kiddie pool. (Standing water attracts.) Avoid perfume and Limburger cheese, which lures the same mosquitoes that love your feet.

Citronella candles help. Wearing light colors and long sleeves does, too. Rubbing your body with fresh lime or hoary basil? Sure, "if you've got no other options," says Joe Conlon of the American Mosquito Control Association.

The best way to kill a mosquito, explains James Brasseur, research professor at the University of Colorado's aerospace engineering department, is to clap, coming at it with both hands. Slapping the insect against your arm is better than swatting in the air, unless you have perfect aim.

But the most fun way to fight mosquitoes: Zap-It! Essentially, a 2,000-volt badminton racket that lets you lounge around on a warm night, fending off mosquitoes like Martina Navratilova at the net.

REPELLENT RECOMMENDATIONS

Use EPA-registered products with less than 40 percent picaridin or DEET, like Sawyer, Off! Deep Woods, or Ultrathon.

Lemon eucalyptus oil–based products work, too (Try Repel sprays).

Avon Skin So Soft? Not so much.

MOUNTAIN LIONS

/ *Also known as: Pumas, cougars,
and the sensible term,* big cat.

FOUND All over the West, most famously in Los Angeles and, increasingly, the Great Plains and Florida. A lone lion recently roamed Tennessee, which is as far east as they've been seen since the nineteenth century. Well, apart from one cat who made its way to Connecticut, only to be killed by a car.

SIZE A little smaller than Arnold Schwarzenegger.

SOUNDS Hisses, growls, chirps (chirps?), but no, no roars, as fierce and real-lion-like as they look. Too bad, as it'd be nice to know when one is coming.

Here's a decent rule of thumb: Wherever there are deer, there are mountain lions (the Northeast excluded, for now). Counting big cats is tricky, says Veronica Yovovich of the Mountain Lion Foundation. "They're elusive and all look alike." No one knows how many there are in the United States these days, but they estimate 30,000. That sounds like a lot of mountain lions, until you remember there are 324 million people.

One of which, by the way—a woman, in Pescadero, California—recently woke at 3 a.m. to a mountain lion *crawling in her bedroom,* where it snatched her fifteen-pound dog off the foot of her bed and slunk off, neither dog nor cat to be seen again. That is a total anomaly, experts say. She was just really unlucky. That, and she left her door open at night, just a crack.

True, mountain lion populations are on the rise in some places, along with the number of attacks, but your odds of ever seeing a mountain lion, let alone being stalked or killed by one, remain ridiculously minimal. As Michelle LaRue, executive director of the Cougar Network, puts it: "You're more likely to win the lottery."

WHAT TO DO

If, one day, you *do* meet a mountain lion on the trail or, uh, in the city (one was spotted roaming San Francisco not long ago), try your best to look big . . . and very much alive. Stand tall. Stare the lion in the eye. Open your coat. Grab your kids, without bending over. Don't run (mountain lions are faster). But don't just stand there, looking scared out of your mind, either; that suggests you are easy prey. (Which, let's be honest, you are.) Instead, intimidate. Wave your arms. Yell. Scream. Throw water bottles, rocks, whatever you've got. If attacked, "Give 'em hell," says Yovovich. Whatever you do, don't lie down or play dead—or they'll eat you for dinner.

BY THE NUMBERS

3: You are three times more likely to be attacked by a mountain lion if you're hiking solo, so stick together.

1: Number of deer a mountain lion kills a week.

1: Number of humans mountain lions kill in the United States a year.

"PLAYING POSSUM" IS A REAL THING
If cornered or attacked, an opossum will freak out and fake its own death: fall down, foam at the mouth, drool, piss, and ooze some gross green liquid. It works! Nothing wants to eat that.

OPOSSUMS

/ *Also known as: Possums, in Australia. (It's an acceptable, if technically incorrect, shorthand here.)*

FOUND In chimneys, attics, and sheds throughout the Midwest, on both coasts, and in Canada.

SIZE Like an average house cat.

SOUNDS Choo, choo, as in a sneeze, not a train. Growls and hisses, too.

They might look like slightly cuter rats, but opossums are actually the closest thing we've got to kangaroos in this country. Opossums: America's only native marsupials!

Maybe that helps you to like them a little more? Or not. As an online commentator in Indianapolis once put it: "It is not possible to love a possum. Unless you're crazy, or another possum, I suppose."

But as far as uninvited pests go, they're the best of the bunch. Hardcore omnivores, they raid trashcans, chicken coops, and fruit trees—but they won't chew wires, rarely attack, and even more rarely carry rabies. Opossums are god's nocturnal gift to gardens, too, devouring snails and slugs. And they're nature's best defense against Lyme disease: one opossum eats 4,000 ticks a week.

The sad news: they don't live long, often bidding farewell to this world beneath the rubber of a tire—or the bottom of a pool.

WHAT TO DO

"Nothing," is the advice of the esteemed Opossum Society of the United States. See one poking around your backyard? Let it be. They're transient, never staying longer than a few days, like a proper guest. If one gets inside, don't bother prodding with a broom; it won't budge. Just politely show it the door. Or blaze the lights and crank up the tunes, anything to let it know it'd be happier elsewhere. Opossums don't run, but they can swim; they're like mini, furry Michael Phelpses. Eventually, though, they'll drown if they can't get out of the water. And then you'll have to fish them out. So leave a raft in the pool or an *opossum ladder* (actual invention, according to Amazon: Skamper-Ramp; free shipping!). Win-win.

Owls talons are said to be as strong as a German shepherd's bite. / The biggest predatory threat to barred owls is great horneds. / Only one person has ever been killed by a great horned owl. (Wait, what?)

OWLS
(GREAT HORNED)

/ *Also known as: Tigers of the sky.*

FOUND In treetops, deserts, swamps, and plenty of city parks.

SIZE Roughly a fourth-grader, with wings spread.

SOUNDS A deep, booming "Hooo-hoo-hoo-hooo."

Of the hundred or so owl species, the great horned has got to be the most intimidating. It has no actual horns, just giant ear tufts that look like horns; big yellow eyes and long, needle-sharp talons; the crazy sci-fi ability to swivel its neck 270 degrees; and dive-bombing skills even a fighter pilot would envy. Which is why they're good nighttime hunters.

Owls eat squirrels, rats, skunks. (Owls are the *only* animals that'll dare to down a skunk.) They'll also scarf down a porcupine, no problem. A Chihuahua named Chico was once swooped up during a walk in Chicago.

Owls are not after humans—but when they're nesting, watch out. Great horned owls are as protective as any helicopter parent at a playground. Barred owls are equally aggressive. As the historically East Coast–only owl expands west, they're increasingly acting out, says David Craig, biology professor at Willamette University. A few years ago, there was a rash of attacks on unsuspecting joggers in a Salem, Oregon, park. Heads were stabbed, caps stolen. "Owlcapone" it was called, and it made national news. In response, Rachel Maddow designed a new kind of yellow caution sign: "angry owl." Thousands of orders came in from around the world, and twenty are still posted around the park.

WHAT TO DO

If you come across an owl's nest, give it space. Wave your arms slowly overhead so the bird sees you but isn't startled. Bang a couple of cans together. Keep little kids close and dogs on leash. Don a hat, with pom-poms preferably, says Craig. (It's more intimidating.) If you're *really* worried, glue big googly eyes to the back of your hat, and the owl will think you're a giant predator. Bike helmets help. An umbrella is even better.

PIGEONS

/ *Also known as: Rats with wings.*

FOUND Pecking around cities and parks everywhere.

SIZE A gravy boat, with feet.

SOUNDS A gurgly cooing.

There's a real love-hate thing going on when it comes to people and pigeons. But unless you're the Bird Woman in Mary Poppins, the Brooklyn artist who goes by Mother Pigeon, or a member of the century-old National Pigeons Association (like Mike Tyson, who has 1,800 of them), it's mostly hate.

Especially if you're Sean Childers, assistant vice president of operations at Texas Tech University, whose department spends $100,000 a year cleaning up after pigeons. It's the campus architecture, Childers explains: Spanish Renaissance, all those eaves and ledges.

The birds roost overnight "and leave a whole mess in the morning," says Childers—twenty-five pounds of mess per pigeon per year, which the grounds crew power washes away six days a week.

Pigeons *can* do more than poop, though. In World War II, rock pigeons really did carry letters for the U.S. Army Signal Corps (it's not just a cartoon). They also helped Charles Darwin—a pigeon lover who studied the differences between wild and captive birds—formulate some aspects of his theory of evolution. But these days, pigeons are less heroic messengers, more human nuisance (hence that "rats with wings" thing). That's why pigeons love living around people—we feed them, whether intentionally or not.

Pigeons mate for life. / They breed at least six times a year. / The population declined 46 percent between 1966 and 2015, according to the North American Breeding Bird Survey, and still they're everywhere: more than 1 million pigeons in New York City alone.

WHAT TO DO

Well, at Texas Tech, Childers roped in PhD candidate Erin Stukenholtz and twenty-three undergrads to count pigeons weekly to help determine the best plan of attack (final tally: 11,500). They've opted to give bird birth control (Ovocontrol) a try. Scatter it like cracked corn, and the birds gobble it up. Otherwise, modifying where they roost is the only humane option, says Stukenholtz. Skip trapping and relocating: "Pigeons will just fly home again."

Hawks help. London's Trafalgar Square has a lot fewer pigeons than it used to now that the city releases birds of prey on a regular basis. So, if you're a falconer, you're in good shape. But if you're just tired of your car getting crapped on. . . . "There's a guy on campus who drives a green Cadillac. Every time he parks, he puts a stuffed owl on his hood," says Stukenholtz. "Never seen a pigeon go near it."

PORCUPINES

/ *Also known as: Quill-pigs, porkies.*

FOUND In forests around New England, the upper Midwest, the West, and Canada.

SIZE As big as a microwave.

SOUNDS Chatter, squeals.

Apart from a porcupine that clung to a skier's leg on the slopes of Alta, Utah, several years ago, porkies usually leave people alone.

Dogs, however, get quilled all the time. Large dogs, like Siberian huskies, Saint Bernards, and German shepherds have it the worst. An off-leash walk in the woods can have them running back looking like an acupuncture appointment gone wrong.

Defensive porcupines get prickly, like people. Slowpokes and totally near-sighted, these extra-large rodents wouldn't stand a chance in the wild if it weren't for the 30,000 four-inch quills hiding beneath their hair, each tipped with hundreds of microscopic, backward-facing barbs that detach upon physical contact. No, they don't shoot. But they do sink ever deeper into the skin, until you pull them out.

WHAT TO DO

If a porcupine comes waddling toward you, walk away slowly, without turning your back. Give it space. Don't give it candy, like skiers in Telluride used to do to a famous local named Stickers. (Stickers eventually had to be relocated because he'd become an aggressive beggar.)

Dogs don't know any better. Quilled once, they'll get quilled again. If there are only a few quills, pull them out yourself. (Coyote Peterson intentionally quilled himself on YouTube just to show 16 million people how.) Use pliers—not fingers—for a firm grip. Don't twist or turn. If they break, they'll embed further. Be quick. Quills can puncture organs. And if your dog suddenly looks more like a sea urchin (see page 113), get her to the vet. Don't DIY. It's less painful for everyone.

HUNGRY FOR PORCUPINE?
Porcupines' quill-free bellies are like caviar to cougars. A hungry mountain lion will flip a porky on his back faster than a McDonald's cook can flip a burger. Some people eat them too. "Fresh roasted porcupine over the campfire is great," claims one outdoorsman online. Although "not as good as beaver."

BUNNIES ARE THE NEW HAMSTERS
At last count, there were 6 million pet rabbits in America. Adopted in a flurry around Easter, the bunnies are often tossed to the wolves (and skunks and foxes) soon after, says Stacey Taylor, who runs the Facebook page "Bunnies Matter in Vegas Too." She advises, "Do your research; rabbits are high-maintenance."

RABBITS

/ *Also known as: Hares, bunnies.*

FOUND Wreaking havoc throughout suburbia.

SIZE A pineapple, but softer.

It's hard not to adore something that bounds around with a fluffy white pom-pom on its butt.

But anyone with a manicured lawn, a penchant for tulips, or a garden full of greens falls out of bunny-love once they realize their backyard has become a salad bar. "Sometimes it takes people awhile to figure it out," says Alison O'Connor, a horticulturalist for Colorado State University Extension who makes house calls. "They're shocked to learn that rabbits can be so destructive."

One yard she surveyed was completely destroyed. "Ten percent grass, the rest was totally dead," says O'Connor. "I told the homeowner it was rabbits, and she was, like, 'No! But they're so cute!'"

Cute lawnmowers that can carry fleas and *tularemia* ("rabbit fever")—which is on the rise, according to the Centers for Disease Control and Prevention. Kentucky Blue Grass is a bunny's favorite meal, but they'll feed on anything, says O'Connor, "and feed and feed."

Suddenly, "eats like a rabbit" only sort of makes sense. Eating is pretty much *all* rabbits do, apart from that other rabbit habit.

WHAT TO DO

Get a beagle and all your bunny issues will go away: the cropped grass, their pellets, that scent of pee. Otherwise, secure fencing is key, says O'Connor, at least two feet tall and buried below ground. Chicken wire won't cut it; they'll slip right through. Instead, buy hardware cloth, staple it to a fence, or bend it into a little cage around each plant. (Not so pretty, but it works.)

Motion sprinklers and products with names like Rabbit Stopper should help for a spell. What about scattering human hair, spraying Tabasco? "Old wives' tales," dismisses O'Connor. Sprinkling fox urine is a better bet. Except it smells like . . . fox urine, she says. "Kind of a turnoff."

BUNNIES IN THE BACKYARD

By Rebecca Flint Marx, food writer and editor

Our dog found the rabbit's nest before we did. An Airedale terrier, he had a better sense of smell than me and my sister. We, however, had a better sense of moral outrage, and as we stood watching Valentine dig up an innocent baby bunny, we screamed at the top of our lungs. I was eight, my sister was seven, and the sight of him shaking this helpless creature by its tiny neck was easily the worst thing ever.

After our mother chased Valentine away, we picked up the dead bunny and gave it a proper coffin. It was too young to have fur, and I still remember the way its soft pink skin felt in my hands. Its own mom was nowhere to be found. I loved all animals, but this felt personal; my dog had murdered Peter Cottontail.

To love rabbits is to love the security of children's books, which is the only place a rabbit gets a happy ending. Loving them in the real world entails knowing the bunny is not long for it, bound to fall prey to a hawk or raccoon, a car tire, or an otherwise typically civilized Airedale terrier.

It didn't occur to me as we prepared our bunny burial that my parents were probably relieved to have one less rabbit in the yard. Like the deer and groundhogs who threatened the crocuses he planted, my father, like most homeowners, regarded rabbits as pests. He later built a fence. But it didn't deter my love for those bunnies. Still today, somewhere in the Michigan soil, there's a shoebox buried with a little piece of my heart.

RACCOONS

/ *Also known as: Masked bandits, night raiders.*

FOUND Roving woods and wetlands around North America and gorging in a garbage can near you.

SIZE Fourteen to twenty pounds; the world's fattest clocked in at seventy-five pounds: Bandit, the pet of a Pennsylvania woman who fed him ice cream and french fries.

SOUNDS Chittering, snarling, screeching.

As rare as raccoon attacks are—once you hear one of these crazy rabid raccoon stories, it sticks with you.*

Not long ago, a pack of a dozen raccoons assaulted a couple walking their dogs in San Francisco. A six-year-old boy in New Jersey was mauled while walking to school with his mom. (He was okay. A kind stranger came to the rescue with a pole and beat the raccoon to death.) A Maine woman was attacked by a rabid raccoon and she drowned it, in a puddle, *with her own hands*.

Far more common, though, than raccoons that tackle are raccoons that raid your trash. And lately they're loving suburbs and, increasingly, cities, where every night it's all-you-can-eat. Especially if you make it easy for them. So don't.

WHAT TO DO

Like Motel 6, leave the light on. Set a radio outside tuned in to National Public Radio. (Just anchor it, or they may walk off with it. True story.) Sprinkle ammonia on each trash bag. They hate the smell as much as we do. Get those heavy-duty bungee cords that snap tightly. String flashing Christmas bulbs around the trash area. It's festive! And it wards them off.

Still, there's only so much you can do. Cat food, water bowls, and dog doors are all welcome mats for raccoons.

Moreover, with their humanlike hands, they can literally turn doorknobs.

If you panic, the raccoon panics. And that makes things worse. So keep calm and help the raccoons move on. Open windows. Make a trail of marshmallows, cheese, or Fig Newtons (apparently they're big fans) to try to lead the rascal outside, banging a broom behind it. Never try to trap one yourself—call animal control. These guys can get aggressive, especially if they've had babies and made your house their home.

*Cue the *This American Life* story, "The Hills Have Eyes." Listen. Or maybe don't . . .

RACCOONS IN THE KITCHEN

By Peter Orner, author of Am I Alone Here?

I had a roommate who cooked: Gary. Nothing gourmet, but
he always had something simmering on the stove; always an
enormous slab of meat in the oven. Always enough for me and
a battalion of the local National Guard. Sometimes he cleaned
up on Saturdays. Some weeks he'd forget altogether.

One night, as I was walking up the stairs, I heard this noise coming
from the kitchen. *Noises*, actually. Baby feet noises? Little gnaw-
gnaw noises? Brazen, carefree noises? I looked in, and there they
were: two gastronomically ecstatic raccoons on the counter.
Striped, food-drunk cuddlies feasting, feasting. Two raccoons
who were not only not afraid of me, the apartment's original
leaseholder, but also stood there staring at me hard, their mouths
still chewing, as if they wanted to see into my soul. What kind of
human was I? Was *I* the purveyor of all this bounty, this sad dude
in a flannel? "You cooked this roast?" they seemed to say.

Ultimately, it didn't matter who was the chef. It was me who
crashed their party in my own kitchen and it was only me they
had eyes for, as if they knew I'd be telling this story for years.
I wondered if they were a couple, husband and wife. She was
bigger than he was. Cheese drooped off her snout.

I grabbed a broom and tried to shoo them off. Neither flinched,
no matter how much I poked. Eventually, they departed on their
own terms, clearly satisfied. If raccoons can saunter, those two
sauntered. He followed her out the door and into the night.

RATS

/ *Also known as: Brown rats, street rats, sewer rats, Norway rats (though they originated in Asia).*

FOUND Rummaging through garbage, sewers, and (hopefully) outside restaurants everywhere, except famously "rat-free" Alberta, Canada.

SIZE A sweet potato with a tail (but not as tasty).

SOUNDS Chattering, hissing, squeaking, shrieking.

Scientists need rats. The rest of us, though, do not. And yet we're overrun. They say there's about one rat per person in the United States. That's a lot of freaking rats.

And it's getting worse. In Chicago and Boston and Manhattan, reports of rats have spiked every year since 2012. Complaints in NYC were up almost 40 percent in the first quarter of 2016 compared to the year prior. They spread dozens of diseases, like hepatitis C and salmonella; they occasionally bite babies; and rats even contribute to depression, according to a recent study. They also eat their own poop, but that's neither here nor there. The question is: What can we do about them? It's a problem people have been trying to figure out since the fourteenth century. (Bubonic plague ring a bell?)

Mayor De Blasio recently put a whopping $32 million toward defeating rats in New York City, including deploying more than 7,000 supposedly rat-proof garbage bins around the city and packing burrows with EPA-approved Rat Ice (dry ice that suffocates the rats with carbon dioxide). Sounds . . . fun.

Do not try this at home. Skip the traditional rat poison, too. It's bad for the environment, other animals, and people, and it just pushes rats into the far depths of your house to die and rot, leaving a stench almost grosser than the rat itself.

WHAT TO DO

Basically, you want to starve the suckers. Take away their water source (rats need to drink ten times their body weight in water a day), fix plumbing leaks, and empty buckets of old rainwater. *Do not leave food lying around.* It's too tempting. Shut them out of your house and seal off any and all entry points. Take the trash out first thing in the morning, in secure bins. Don't just leave plastic bags on the curb (ahem, Manhattan); that's basically saying, "Come on in!" And, please, for so many reasons, pick up your dog's poop. (Yeah, rats eat dog poop, too.)

You could try setting snap traps (see Mice, page 77) with peanut butter or bacon grease or burger meat, but do you really want to deal with the aftermath? When it comes to rats, you'd be wise to leave it to the professionals.

But real rat relief may be on the way, thanks to a new technology called ContraPest: contraception for rats! Brilliant. Sustainable. Humane. It's been tested by the New York Metropolitan Transit Authority and Housing Authority and pest control pros coast to coast. An over-the-counter pill for you? Perhaps eventually.

CONTINUED

RATS 101

For a real education, there's an actual Rodent Academy, in—where else?—New York. It's dedicated to imparting rat-management wisdom to pest-control professionals and homeowners around the country. One of the many things you can learn at rat school: if you see droppings or grease smudges or chewed wires—or your dog staring blankly at the wall—there's a good chance you've got rats. Plural, always.

RAT FICTION?

Rat kings: A few dozen rats whose tails are knotted together in cold spaces to form one giant swirling ratty mass, meant to help keep them warm. True, or cryptozoology . . . you decide.

Rats *can* swim up your toilet. / They have sex for pleasure, too, a lot of sex. (Female rats can mate up to 500 times in a six-hour period.) / Two rats mating, over an eight- to twelve-month life span, will generate 15,000 descendants. Ew.

RATS IN THE BEDROOM

By Diana Kapp, writer and runner

I think the word is *infestation*. It's never a good word. Especially when it's used by Rocky, my Rat Guy, whose phone number I have memorized. A feat in our smartphone age.

Three years ago, the city tore down a raised freeway behind my house, in San Francisco, turning the neighborhood into a never-ending construction zone. Rats, Rocky told me, love construction zones.

Why they chose *my* house, I have no clue. "I'm sooo sorry!" neighbors sympathized, smugly. Things escalated quickly, while my husband was out of town, of course. One fat, long-tailed rat raiding the cracker cabinet became an entire crew scurrying inside the wall behind my bed.

Two nights later, holy crap, they hit the closet. I woke to rummaging followed by a thump: a blue suede sandal knocked to the floor. I raced to my daughter's room.

The next day, I treated my bedroom like a crime scene. Except eventually, I needed my sneakers. Stomping toward the bedroom door, I flung the closet open. No rats, but strewn across the room was their aftermath: grayish shreds, mixed with a tan-tinted-something of a different texture, like chopped-up rubber bands as if a buzz saw had been through. The nightstand drawer was open so wide, it was hanging.

The rats had come, like teenagers searching for an extra $10, and instead found a Pleasure Pack of Trojans, fifty or so. Each condom madly chewed in pursuit of lube.

I swear they weren't flavored.

RATTLESNAKES

/ Also known as: Rattlers.

FOUND In the Southwest; there are thirteen species in Arizona alone.

SIZE When outstretched, as long as an NBA player is tall.

SOUNDS Hisssssss, rattle-rattle.

Stuff of nightmares: A four-year-old in Texas recently found a rattlesnake in his toilet. Smart boy called for his mom. She killed it. Then Big Country Snake Removal came over—and found twenty-three more.

Luckily, most people see rattlesnakes outside, on the trail, under a rock. And most people scream. A fascinating website called Fearof.net ranks fear of snakes, ophiodiophobia, second of all phobias, just behind spiders and above . . . everything else: Heights, public speaking, belly buttons (*omphalophobia*; it's a thing). Kids, though, love snakes. And 1,300 kids get bitten every year, about half by rattlers, with copperhead bites on the rise.

Beyond the usual dizziness, fever, and fang marks that are symptoms of a snake bite, Dr. Steve Curry of Banner Poison Control Center in Phoenix, Arizona, has occasionally witnessed people collapsing within minutes after their throat swelled and cut off breathing.

But the good news: According to the Centers for Disease Control and Prevention, of the 7,000 people in the United States bitten by venomous snakes each year, only about 0.2 percent of bites end in death. Still.

Life span: Ten to twenty-five years. /
Meal plan: One mouse every two weeks.

WHAT TO DO

Leave a snake alone. The bad stuff happens when people don't. Let it pass. Give it a good fifteen feet. Coiled, rattling, and head raised? Give it even more. If you accidentally step on one and get bitten: keep cool. (Uh, OK?) But seriously, don't run; getting your heart rate up makes the venom seep faster. Skip the snakebite kits and tourniquets; that's outdated advice. Just call Poison Control at 800-222-1222 ASAP. In Arizona or California—where most bites occur—plug this number into your phone.

And do your best to avoid them in the first place. A sunny, 90°F day is snake weather. No flip-flops, wear boots. Jeans, even. (A study actually proved denim's effectiveness against venom injection.) Don't use earbuds (you want to hear the rattle). On a mountain bike, be extra cautious. Rattlesnakes are designed to hear the pounding of bison hooves, not the quiet roll of a tire tread. Peek under a log before sitting on it. Shake out your sleeping bag. And if you've got to peel off the trail to pee, toss a few pebbles first.

SEAGULLS

/ *Also known as: Rats of the ocean, gulls.*

FOUND Stealing food up and down the coasts and, increasingly, in cities.

SIZE As varied as designer handbags.

Seagulls are bold birds and getting bolder. They've always pranced around beach picnics and pooped on piers—but now they're swooping up sandwiches right *out of our hands.* They've even been known to stroll into stores to help themselves to snacks: like Sam, of Scotland, who pinched a bag of Tangy Cheese Doritos every day for a month, becoming an early online sensation.

"I once came out of a donut shop on Mackinac Island and had a seagull hovering off my shoulder for three blocks," says Elizabeth Wheeler Alm, microbiologist at Central Michigan University in the Great Lakes region, where the number of gulls has gone up dramatically.

In Ocean City, New Jersey, too, seagulls have gotten so aggressive that the mayor declared a $500 fine and ninety days of imprisonment for anyone found intentionally feeding them. No one's gone to jail yet for seagull crimes, but the message—blared over loudspeakers along the boardwalk—has been getting through . . . to everyone, it seems, but the birds. A local pizza shop owner said that in one week, he gave out sixty-two free slices to customers who'd had theirs swiped. (Very sweet. He didn't have to.)

WHAT TO DO

If you've got a beach house, get a sheepdog. Wheeler found walking a sheepdog along the beach at dawn and dusk reduced the number of seagulls by 99 percent.

Everyone else, resist the urge to cart the entire contents of your refrigerator to the beach. It's debatable whether a red beach blanket wards them off, but it's worth a try. You might as well bring a squirt gun, too. But the only way to deter them in the long run is to, you know, stop adding your garbage to already overflowing outdoor trashcans.

A recent study out of the Netherlands concluded that the true source of seagull-human conflict is the sheer availability of human food. *Please do not feed the birds.* Keep whatever you've got in the cooler until lunchtime. And screw etiquette—scarf it down.

A HITCHCOCKIAN ISSUE
Every season, San Francisco's AT&T Park gets
literally swarmed by seagulls. During the seventh
or eighth inning, they start swooping for fans'
leftover garlic fries. (Somehow they must sense
that the stadium will soon clear out.)

Sea urchins have no actual face, just a mouth and an anus. / Some sea urchins live for two hundred years. / All urchins taste better than they feel.

SEA URCHINS

/ *Also known as: Porcupines of the sea, wana, Hawaiian tattoos.*

FOUND All oceans; all climates.

SIZE A softball, covered in needles.

Gastronomes go nuts for what's inside a sea urchin—that creamy, pricey delicacy known as *uni*. (You know you're eating gonads, right?)

Sea urchins know they've got something worth protecting, so mess with one and you'll suffer the consequences: sharp spines that can puncture through a neoprene booty and send shooting pain and, sometimes, but not always, poison into your body.

"It's excruuuuciatingly painful," says underwater photographer Deron Verbeck, who once found the entire sole of his right foot covered with quills. "I was paddling and crying back to shore." Ouch. But not as bad as what could've followed—puking, paralysis, respiratory distress. In the event of which, call 911. Going untreated could cause nerve damage and arthritis.

"Sea urchins are one of the top ocean hazards for sure," says Kirk Ziegler, a longtime lifeguard on Oahu's North Shore. Snorkelers, swimmers, divers, waders—urchins don't discriminate. "Tourists are stupidly tramping all over the reef or trying to stand on the rocky bottom. Then they come running out, yelling 'I'm gonna die! I'm gonna die!'" (probably not) with stings on their feet, on their hands. Verbeck once witnessed a man somehow get stung . . . on his tush.

WHAT TO DO

"I told that guy to get his wife to pee on it," laughs Verbeck. "I've seen it work!" (Debatable.) What definitely doesn't work is pulling out the quills. "Too brittle; they just disintegrate," he says. Tweezers don't do much.

Soaking in vinegar, or superhot water with a little Epsom salt, helps the spines soften. Otherwise, "there's really nothing you can do," says Verbeck. "You just gotta wait it out." Eventually, either your body will absorb the spines or whatever's embedded will work its way to the surface. Ultimately, you'll be left with little inky dots all over your foot, like it's been tattooed for fun. (Hardly.)

SHARKS

/ *Also known as: Man-eaters,*
albeit unfairly, say experts.

FOUND In every ocean, shallow water included. "If you've been in the water, you've been within ten feet of a shark," says George Burgess, director of shark research at the University of Florida. "I guarantee it."

SIZE L to XXXXL.

SOUNDS *Silent.*

"The fear of sharks is way overblown," says Hawaii-based underwater photographer Deron Verbeck (see Sea Urchins, page 113). He swims with them. Like, regularly. While most of humanity hopes to avoid ever encountering a great white, this guy lives for it. Remember Werner Herzog's haunting documentary of fearless bear-lover Timothy Treadwell? Verbeck is like the "Grizzly Man" of sharks, if slightly less insane. When he sees a shark in the water, he jumps in—and gets as close as he can, camera in hand.

And more and more, he's bringing people in with him—normal people, he says. "Cruise-ship kind of people." Indeed, swimming with sharks (*sans* cage) is suddenly a tourist activity on par with paragliding. Blame it on social media, on the Discovery Channel's *Shark Week*, or on Verbeck's otherworldly unthreatening photos, but shark anxiety seems to be subsiding—at least for some people.

In a way, this is a good thing, as the stats just don't support the craziness. In 2016, there were four fatalities *worldwide*. Your odds of being killed by a shark are, according to Burgess, "as close to zero as you can get": About a 1 in 3,748,067 chance during your lifetime according to the Florida Museum of Natural History. There are bigger fatal beach hazards to worry about: drowning (1 in 1,134 chance); sun/heat exposure (1 in 13,729); driving *to* the beach (1 in 84).

However, white shark populations are rising, says Burgess, as are the populations of the seals they eat. Thanks, Marine Mammal Protection Act. And sharks are returning to their roots, reclaiming beaches where we've merely been squatting—from north of Los Angeles up through Washington, and specifically Cape Cod. In the face of global warming, Burgess predicts we'll start seeing great whites in British Columbia and Alaska before long and more frequent encounters on the Cape, where sharks are a cottage industry. "Shark tees, shark cocktails, shark music festivals," says Burgess. "What they haven't had—since 1936—is a fatal shark attack." Last summer, one came close: biting a paddleboard, but not the person on it. "It's time to start anticipating who we're rubbing elbows with."

CONTINUED

WHAT TO DO

Whatever Verbeck does. In the twenty-five years he's (voluntarily) been circled by sharks, he's never once been chomped. He's had two very close calls, though. Both times the sharks rushed him—and both times he played the aggressor, pounding the shark on its sensitive snout with his camera, and it retreated. Burgess backs that up. "Punch it on the snout, then swim like hell."

Any shark that reaches six feet in length is potentially dangerous, says Burgess. And the most dangerous ones—white, tiger, and bull sharks—all come into shallow waters, so watch out.

The real secret to survival is not panicking, says Verbeck. If a shark comes around, huddle back-to-back with whoever's nearby. Don't start splashing or going crazy. "Be still, let it swim to you—and then make a movement toward it," he says. It's counterintuitive, Verbeck admits; your instinct is to flee, not swim *right at* it. "But that's what you've got to do."

If it does take a bite, battle. Poke its eyes, claw its gills. Basically, the goal, as Verbeck puts it, is to "stay alive."

As for the "shark repellents" on the market—Shark Shield, No Shark, Shark Shocker—they are not worth the money, says Burgess.

HOW TO AVOID SHARKS IN THE FIRST PLACE

Swim in groups. Wear a light-colored suit so you don't look like a seal. (Why are wetsuits always black? wonders Burgess, who'd design *his* light on the belly, like a fish, so as to disappear in the sunlight when the shark looks up.)

And because you're curious: menstruating women "might be attractive" to sharks, says Burgess, but there's been no solid data supporting an increase of attacks. But, he says, "If one is attempting to maximize the reduction of risks, it is one thing that can be avoided." (Good to know.)

And unless you're as crazy as Verbeck: If you see a shark in the water, it's simple— calmly get out.

SHARK STATS

52 million: Americans who swim in the ocean every year.

1: Americans, on average, who die from a shark attack every year. (Not to say there are no unprovoked attacks, though: In the United States in 2016 there were forty-three; in 2015 there were fifty-nine. 40 to 50 percent of all unprovoked shark attacks in America occur in the Sunshine State.)

6: People killed by sharks worldwide a year.

70 million: Sharks killed by people a year. "So who's the attacker," asks Burgess, "and who's the attacked?"

SHEEP

/ *Also known as: Ewes, lambs, rams.*

FOUND Peacefully grazing in pastures and public lands for centuries.

SIZE A big fluffy beanbag chair, at best. A frail, fleshy old man at worst.

"Oh, people encounter sheep all the time," says Renee Catherin of the Ketchum Ranger District in the Sawtooth National Forest—in Idaho, Texas, Wyoming, Colorado, rural California. There are 5.2 million head of domestic sheep in the United States—you're bound to bump into them eventually, by the hundreds if not thousands.

You'll likely be in your car, in a rush, when you are stopped by the fluffiest of traffic jams. Or it will happen when you're out hiking, in which case, it's not the sheep you need to worry about. "Sheep are the most submissive creatures ever created," says Catherin. It's the Great Pyrenees guarding them against the mountain lions and coyotes that'd otherwise take 'em down.

Dog walkers: Take extra caution. A guard dog can't distinguish between your yellow lab and a lone wolf, says Catherin. "They're hardwired to go after any canine." In 2008, two Great Pyrenees even went after a competitive cyclist in Colorado. It wasn't pretty.

WHAT TO DO

On a bike, get off. And quietly walk it around the sheep. You might not see any guard dogs at first, but they're there somewhere. And when they come for you, don't scream or throw your water bottle; just be still and hope for the best. On foot, move slowly, in a "determined fashion," says Catherin. Never cut through the center of a flock, fun as it sounds.

On the road, defer to the official drivers' handbook of New Zealand, famously home to more sheep than people: "Pull over until the animals have moved past you." Patience. At night, turn off your headlights and creep gradually; they'll still see you.

If you hit a sheep? You'll owe the rancher several hundred bucks per animal. (It's cheaper than crashing into a cow, but still.)

And never honk at a herd; that's just mean.

WHAT ABOUT BIGHORNS?

For the most part, they prefer rocky cliffs you can't handle. But they *will* descend, so drive carefully. In Utah, one bighorn recently chased a group of golfers and rammed a garage. But that's rare.

BEST REMEDY IF *YOU* GET SPRAYED
"Time" says Jerry Dragoo, of the Dragoo Institute for the Betterment of Skunks and Skunk Reputations. He's been sprayed a lot—nine times in eleven seconds by one skunk alone. "I used to just take a shower," he says. "That doesn't work." What about tomato juice? Hogwash, he says. It just makes you smell like tomato juice, too.

SKUNKS

/ *Also known as: Essence peddlers, fart squirrels.*

FOUND Everywhere but Hawaii and Alaska.

SIZE A bowling ball with a bushy ponytail.

PBS has a unique kind of content warning: "This video will include slow-motion footage of skunk anuses," cautions Anna Rothschild, host of the web series "Gross Science." Viewer discretion is kind of valid, as once you see what a skunk butt spewing a greenish, oily, sulfur-containing liquid actually looks like, there's no unseeing it.

Unfortunately, our odds of bumping into a beady-eyed, black-and-white-striped omnivore are increasing as we continue to horn in on their turf, with our trash, uncleaned grills, and lazy house maintenance.

Skunks have few predators, as coyotes, foxes, and even grizzlies know to stay away. And so they scamper around, proliferating freely, their bushy tails poised for any threat: couples on an evening stroll, kids in the yard, dogs off-leash. Poor climbers and slow runners, a skunk's only self-defense is its stench.

WHAT TO DO

"Treat a skunk like it's an African lion," advises Mark Vargas of the Oregon Department of Fish and Wildlife. "Don't startle it. Let it have its way, and it'll mosey off."

If it doesn't . . . you spray first. Hose it. Otherwise, once a skunk arches its back, lifts its tail, and starts hissing and stomping (spotted skunks will do this impressive headstand move), you're out of luck. With a fifteen-foot spray and impeccable aim, skunks can leave you nauseous, temporarily blind, and reeking for a couple of days; your pet, a couple of weeks; and your house, a couple of *years*.

Best remedy for pets: Bathe them in 1 quart of 3 percent hydrogen peroxide (available at drugstores), ¼ cup baking soda, and 1 teaspoon liquid pet shampoo. / Best remedy for your house: Uh, a guy in a 4,000 square-foot place in Pennsylvania had to move out.

SQUIRRELS

/ *Also known as: Rats with fluffy tails, road kill.*

FOUND Squirreling around wherever there are trees.

SIZE Bigger than a chipmunk, smaller than a bunny.

A lot of people like squirrels, like, *really* like squirrels. Karelia Dubkowksi, an art teacher in Boise, Idaho, dresses them in miniature tiaras, top hats, and Groucho Marx glasses. Her squirrels aren't pets per se, just wild rodents she invites over for play dates, then sends back to the woods. Adam Pearl's squirrel, Joey, would sleep over. Adam and Joey also lived in Idaho, together; Joey recently scared off a burglar, and the local news went nuts. (Joey later moved out, but not after cuddling up to Adam to say good-bye.) It sounds ridiculous, but start following Jill the Squirrel's Instagram (@this_girl_is_a_squirrel, with half a million fans), and suddenly you'll want a cute little squirrel, too.

Unless you're a gardener. "Squirrels suck," says Johanna Silver, garden editor of *Sunset* magazine. "What goes on between me and squirrels? Hatred." They dig up soil. Snack on tulips. And devour tomatoes. "They wait until a tomato is perfectly ripe—then snag it, just before me," says Silver. "I swear they make eye contact, too, right before pilfering."

WHAT TO DO

Lively online gardening forums offer all sorts of solutions. Sprinkling PredatorPee sounds promising. (Wolf, coyote, bobcat piss—take your pick.) Scattering dog hair, or your own hair, supposedly helps, too (if you need a cut anyway). Shrouding crops in wire caging is effective if secured really well, says Silver, as is spraying a cayenne pepper–based concoction around your garden or dusting it with chili powder.

Meanwhile, plant more daffodils. Squirrels don't dig 'em. You could always get a cat. But then you've got a different kind of squirrel problem.

POWER HUNGRY

"Squirrels have taken down the electrical power grid more times than the zero times hackers have," Peter W. Singer, of the Brookings Institution, once said. That's almost 900 times since 1987, according to Cyber Squirrel 1, which tracks these things.

SENIOR MOMENT

In 2016, a squirrel also took down a trio of old folks at a Florida retirement community. There was biting and scratching, until eventually someone threw the squirrel outside.

STINGRAYS

/ *Also known as:*
Pancakes of the sea.

FOUND Hiding in shallow coastal waters, under the sand.

SIZE From a dinner plate on up (in Thailand, as big as a trampoline).

"Whenever you get feet in the water and stingrays where the feet are, you get problems," says Mike Halphide, a longtime lifeguard in Newport Beach, California. With warmer weather and more people going to the beach in general, we're seeing more stingray attacks, says Halphide.

Stingrays sit around like lazy teenagers, heads partially buried in the sand, chowing down on sand crabs and moving only when the tide makes them. That means that on calm, warm days at low tide, Halphide is on the lookout for people hopping out of the ocean on one leg, wincing.

A ray's sting is painful. But "most people have no complications," Dr. Carl Schulz of the University of California, Irvine, recently concluded, after two years researching attacks at Seal Beach—the Stingray Capital of the World.

Step on a ray, and it'll whip up its barbed tail filled with venom. At first, it feels like a pencil poke, and then it ramps way up. "Can't speak to this personally," says Halphide, "but my friend said it hurt more than childbirth."

WHAT TO DO

To avoid rays in the first place, do the Stingray Shuffle, says Halphide. Wiggle and drag your feet as you enter the water. Kicking up sand lets the rays know you're coming, and they'll skedaddle. If you still manage to step on one, there's nothing you can do but soak your foot in superhot water until the pain eventually subsides.

Lifeguard stations in Orange County have buckets of hot water waiting, with chairs. It looks like a lineup of people getting pedicures, says Halphide, "miserable pedicures."

The most famous people to die by stingray (and some of the *only* people to die by stingray): Australia's Steve Irwin (stabbed in the chest) and Odysseus (killed by his son with a spear tipped with its venomous spine). / According to TripAdvisor, seeing "Stingray City" is the number 1 of 167 things to do on Grand Cayman, where people pay to pet, feed, and kiss stingrays. "Sounds horrifying to me," says Halphide, "but my mother-in-law loved it."

TICKS

/ Also known as: Deer ticks,
blacklegged ticks.

FOUND Concentrated in the Northeast, where one or two of every three ticks is infected with Lyme disease.

SIZE Ranging from a poppy seed to a sesame seed.

Lying in the grass on a summer day used to be the epitome of carefree— now it comes with a level of anxiety formerly reserved for real dangers, like choking on steak, or nuclear war.

Ticks are everywhere, literally waiting for us. They can't jump or fly. Instead, they cling to the tips of grasses and shrubs, upper legs outstretched, ready to latch on to whoever happens to come by.

When a tick needs a host, it finds one—a squirrel, a deer, your dad—they climb aboard, and start sucking blood. Slowly. Until caught. The longer they suck, the greater the risk of getting Lyme disease, which causes fever, fatigue, arthritis, and paralysis—and affects 300,000 people in the United States, a number that has more than doubled since 2001.

WHAT TO DO

Start with a nightly, stripped-down, scalp-to-toe tick check all summer long. Get in there. Ticks hide. They also hitchhike home on clothes, pets, and backpacks. So wash everything on high heat—then bathe (within two hours, says the Centers for Disease Control and Prevention). It takes a tick twenty-four to thirty-six hours to get comfy and infect you, so search and seize ASAP.

Don't use your fingers to remove a tick. You'll just crush it, and it'll spew its guts, and you'll have a greater risk of getting whatever it's got. Use tweezers. Pull upward with steady pressure; it'll pop out. Wash the bite, flush the tick down the toilet, and if you're in prime Lyme disease territory, for the next month, look for red splotches, a bull's-eye rash, and any symptoms. If you catch Lyme disease early, it's totally treatable.

DEER DON'T DESERVE ALL THE BLAME
Mice and ticks are tight, too. Felicia Keesing, an ecologist with the New York–based Tick Project, found that more mice means more Lyme disease. According to Keesing, mice infect 95 percent of ticks that feed on them. And one mouse might have fifty to one hundred ticks on its face.

CHECK EVERYWHERE
Tony Goldberg, a pathobiologist at the University of Wisconsin School of Veterinary Medicine in Madison, found a tick up his nose—twice. Retrieving it took long forceps, a mirror, and flashlight. Fun.

U.S. turkey consumption has increased 104 percent since 1970. / Wild turkeys sleep in oak trees. / Male wild turkeys provide zero parental care.

TURKEYS

/ *Also known as:*
Thanksgiving dinner.

FOUND In forests and farmland, and puttering outside people's doors.

SIZE A solid preschooler.

Until recently, the average American encountered turkeys in two forms: between two slices of bread or stuffed, next to the mashed potatoes. Increasingly, though, people are finding them live, in their impressively fanned-out feathered flesh.

Turkeys have been seen chasing cyclists, harassing kids, and pecking mailmen on their morning routes. A fowl in Davis, California, known as Downtown Tom, who frequented the Wells Fargo parking lot, got so aggressive that people called 911, pleading for help. And not long ago, a family was sitting down to dinner in Teaneck, New Jersey, when a massive, muddy bird crashed through the window and landed on the table. (Turns out, a turkey may respond aggressively to its own reflection, thinking it's an intruding turkey. Turkeys: Dumber than they look?)

Coast to coast, and especially in the Midwest, wild turkey populations are on the rise. After being hunted to near extinction (fifty years ago, the United States had just a half-million left), today there are 7 million. "Urbanized wild turkeys are habituated," says John McNerney, a wildlife resource specialist in Davis, California. "They show little fear of humans."

Local newscasters, happy to have a lighthearted tidbit to close out their nightly segment, always report turkey trouble with a smile. But the people turkeys affect are actually pretty traumatized. The mom with the live turkey on her table told reporters: "We got up and literally ran for our lives."

WHAT TO DO

If confronted by a turkey or a flock, tell them who you are: someone who will not be intimidated by a *turkey,* for crying out loud (even though you totally are). McNerney says: Clap and shout; don't run, but walk calmly past. Use an umbrella or a handbag to shoo it off. In Teaneck, a health officer passes out free air horns. They're a little noisy, but it's helped. And if wild turkeys start running after you—at 25 mph—duck inside.

WHALES

/ *Also known as: Moby-Dick.*

> SIZE Humpbacks are sixty feet long and weigh forty tons; blue whales are three times longer than a double-decker bus.

Whale watching is a $2 billion industry, as big as the whales themselves, and getting bigger.

The trips are typically safe—apart from that, uh, recent sinking incident off Vancouver Island. They're also a cattle call: dozens of people packed on a three-hour tour, suppressing nausea, sipping Heinekens, and shuffling side-to-side, cameras pointed at the sea, waiting for a sighting, a spouting, a breach.

Lately, though, people are looking for a more intimate whale experience, without the crowds and cruise ships, says Kate Spencer, captain of the six-person Fast Raft in Monterey Bay. She knows what she's doing. You—tooling around the open ocean on an inflatable Costco kayak intended for ponds—*do not.*

"Kayaking used to be a niche thing," she says. Now they're available to buy or rent anywhere—by anyone. Spencer recently saw a humpback that breached and toppled a tandem kayak with one flip of its fifteen-foot tail. She also regularly sees paddlers playing *National Geographic* with their smartphones. "People forget those images are taken by wildlife photographers with telephoto lenses," says Spencer. "If *you're* getting a pic that close, you're too close."

Paddle boarders, especially, she says, stupidly seek out whales—and then narrowly miss their tails. "We're just waiting for someone to seriously get hurt. Everyone wants an intimate encounter with a whale," says Spencer. "If you really want acknowledgment from an animal, get a dog."

Killer whales may kill walruses, penguins, and other whales—but they don't kill people (well, except for that time at Sea World).

WHAT TO DO

Never startle a whale. Move slowly. Stay at least 100 yards away.

"Always let them come to you," adds British Columbia–based whale expert Brandon Harvey. "Never approach first." It's called harassment, and it's illegal.

If a whale is coming too close, start drumming on the side of your kayak, says Spencer. Otherwise the whale may not hear you. It may see you, but think you're a sea lion. (Whales likely don't see color.) Link up kayaks to look larger. You'll still look like an ant to a whale, but whatever.

Whales have bad moods and prickly personalities, like people. "But they aren't going to eat you," says Spencer. They might charge, though. Imagine a forty-ton truck on the loose underwater.

WILD BOARS

/ *Also known as: Wild pigs, razorbacks, feral free-range swine, nature's bulldozers.*

FOUND Multiplying all over most states these days. California, the Southeast, and Texas—home to half of 'em—have it the worst.

SIZE About as heavy as a middleweight sumo wrestler.

A wild pig is no Wilbur. Lovable these invasive nuisances are not. They are more destructive than one hundred high schoolers at a house party: doing $1.5 billion worth of property and environmental destruction annually. A few years ago, the U.S. Department of Agriculture put $20 million toward defeating them. And still, the pigs are winning.

Hairy and hulking, wild pigs travel in *sounders* of up to one hundred animals. They are always hungry, capable of putting back everything from pecans to entire carcasses. They've got sharp tusks, a 30-mph charge, and the ability to transmit a bunch of diseases. And there are *7 million* of them in America. Gross.

"The wild pig is the most prolific large mammal on the face of Earth," says Dr. Billy Higginbotham, wildlife specialist at Texas A&M. One pumps out a litter of five or six pigs at least once a year. Put another way: "They put my Czechoslovakian grandmother to shame," says Nick Dornak, who heads the lauded Feral Hog Task Force in Caldwell County, Texas, where wild pig dung has done a number on the local water quality.

This is why some people don't feel all that guilty about hunting them, especially when they get paid to. (One hefty hog can fetch as much as $300, plus $5 a tail in Caldwell County—"proof of death," says Dornak, whose county has collected 11,000 of them in three years.) And especially when they love to eat them (wild boar ragu!). Epic's new wild boar bars—made from Texas's feral pigs, per the fine print—are like the new Clif Bar for carnivores. Trap or shoot away! Stricken communities say.

Hunters need to be on hog alert, as do suburban homeowners who love their lawns. Hikers too, though the likelihood of actually being charged is low. You're more likely to crash into one with your car. (Still, seven people a year worldwide are pummeled by a wild pig.)

WHAT TO DO

If you live in Caldwell County, call Dornak, he'll dispatch one of his "big, fancy" $3,000 wireless traps—thirty feet wide, six feet tall, with a six-foot-wide gate—filled with corn, scraps, or raspberry Jell-O. And then he'll wait for the "you've got pigs" ping on his phone at 3:00 a.m. The other option? "Stand on your porch with a shotgun," he says.

But if you're just out for a walk in the woods and are suddenly approached by a sounder, stay cool. They'll probably turn away. If not, climb a tree—and get at least six feet high or they'll climb after you. If charged, sidestep it. (Clearly, this is easier said than done.) Otherwise, you've got no choice but to fight back, while standing. You do not want to get knocked down.

CONTINUED

QUICK AND DIRTY

Most wild pig attacks on humans are done in under a minute. And are
extremely rare. You have less than a one in a million chance of being
assaulted by a wild pig, according to John Mayer at the Savannah
River National Laboratory, who studies them. "This is nothing to lose
sleep over. I would suggest worrying more about bears" (see page 18).

WHY SO MANY WILD BOAR?

They breed like . . . rabbits (see page 95). And they've got no predators.
"There aren't enough mountain lions to make a difference," says Dornak.
"We're the only thing that can keep them in check, and we're losing."

BRINGING HOME THE BACON

"Do you want to buzz droves of hogs fifteen feet off the ground at highway
speeds?" asks the website for a Texas-based company called HeliBacon.
"All you need is a hunting license and a trigger finger!" It's called *aerial
depredation*, also known as hog hunting by helicopter, and lately hedge-fund
managers and millionaires are finding it to be very fun . . . $4,000 for two hours
in the "pork chopper" worth of fun.

WOLVES

/ *Also known as: Big, Bad . . . ; Akela.*

FOUND Mostly in Yellowstone National Park, Alaska, and Canada, and on the rise elsewhere.

SIZE Bigger than a coyote, smaller than a sheep. (But that doesn't stop 'em.)

First of all, let's be real: you'll likely never see a wolf unless you're, say, on a safari in Yellowstone specifically to do so. And even then, a sighting isn't guaranteed. "Some rangers spend their entire careers hoping to see a wolf and never do," says Lorna Smith, executive director of Western Wildlife Outreach, who has seen more than one hundred in her thirty-five-year career. (It's her job; so she knows where to find them.)

After near-extermination, gray wolves have been making a bit of a comeback in recent decades, thanks to protection under the Endangered Species Act. Controversially delisted in some states, there are now some 5,500 gray wolves in the Lower 48; 11,000 in Alaska; and 60,000 in Canada, one of which, according to local reports, recently made off with a loaf of bread from a campsite in Banff.

Not good: According to Doug Smith, a wildlife biologist at Yellowstone, the only attacks on humans "in the entire twentieth century" were by habituated, fed wolves. No thanks to loggers and pipeline workers sharing their lunches.

Although there is one case, not too long ago, of a woman who was killed by a wolf pack while jogging southwest of Anchorage. "She was wearing her headphones!" says Lorna. "We always tell people: Be situationally aware." A wolf will never attack a human on its first encounter with one. (Bears, see page 18, and mountain lions, see page 84, are a different story.)

WHAT TO DO

Even rarer than seeing a wolf, would be being attacked by one. Wolves want nothing to do with you. They're scared of people, and the goal is to keep it that way. "So sound human," advises Lorna.

"Use your voice. Yell. Throw rocks. Look big. Never turn your back on a wolf or on any predator. You want to know where it is." And with wolves, definitely don't run. "You could try climbing a tree?" she offers. "But that's never a very good option."

HISTORIC FLIGHT DELAY
In 1995, a flock of northern flickers grounded the space shuttle *Discovery* by drilling holes in the fuel tank. NASA "pecker checkers" rigged "predator eye" balloons and plastic owls, and played tapes of hooting great horned owls to deter further damage. It worked.

WOODPECKERS

/ *Also known as: Nature's jackhammers, Woody.*

FOUND Tapping on tree trunks and sides of houses, irritating people everywhere.

SIZE As small as a teacup, as large as a crow.

"I HATE YOU. JUST DIE," a Chicago woman has screamed every morning—for close to a decade—at the woodpecker duo outside her bedroom window. She pounds the walls, bang pots, shoots rubber bands. Critter Control once came and blew up a bunch of inflatable owls—that didn't do much. "I just became a crazy bird lady," she says. Woodpeckers are federally protected, so no, you can't just shoot them (to the chagrin of some perturbed people online), not without a special permit at least.

Pileated, red-bellied, the northern flicker—they all peck, from dawn on, hammering their beak at 15 mph, 20 times per second, about 12,000 times a day. They do it to establish their turf, turn on chicks, and dig for insects. And when they start excavating chambers to roost, chiseling away like Geppetto, they turn trees, telephone poles, and house siding (cedar, redwood, even metal) into Swiss cheese.

Damage aside, the drilling drives people insane, during the springtime especially (mating season and all).

WHAT TO DO

Get to the source—as you soon as you hear it, before the bird sets up shop. Inhibit their access to whatever it is they're hammering, and peace and quiet might follow. You can try bird netting, but that's boring. Better would be yarn bombing! It looks cool and seems to curtail the problem, says yarn bomber London Kaye, a street artist who crochets on everything from chain-link fences to mailboxes to tree trunks. Or build them a woodpecker house of their own, and they'll realize that pummeling a tree all day is too much work.

You could paint your house hot pink; supposedly they hate it. Otherwise, deploy an arsenal of scare tactics and don't let up: throw tennis balls—near them, not *at* them. (That's illegal; sorry.) Startle them with their own reflection by dangling mirrors or old CDs. Wind chimes help, until those start to annoy you, too.

ANIMALS FROM MOST TO LEAST DEADLY

This is the approximate number of people killed in the United States per animal, per year. Take heed, it's not bears, sharks, and gators at the top of the list. (Just deer, dogs, and bees?) Still, the good news: Of all human deaths each year, animals cause only about 0.008 percent. (Note to self and readers: Love animals. Don't fear them.)

DEER: 200

BEES, WASPS, AND HORNETS: 60

DOGS: 20 TO 30

COWS: ABOUT 20

HORSES: 20

SNAKES: 5

BEARS: 1

SHARKS: 1

ALLIGATORS: FEWER THAN 1

MOUNTAIN LIONS: FEWER THAN 1

COYOTES: FEWER THAN 1

BLACK WIDOWS: FEWER THAN 1

ACKNOWLEDGMENTS

"Wait, what are we supposed to do again if we run into a bear?" I asked my friend Mandi Bateman one day in the woods. "What about a mountain lion?" "I don't know . . . " she replied, "but that would make a good book!" Thank you, Mandi. Now we know.

Thank you to my work/hotel wife, Bonnie Tsui, who one tipsy eve, wandering wine country, convinced me to write up a proposal. Thank you to smart and savvy Danielle Svetcov, who has been a supporter from the start and at every step of the way. Thank you to the entire Ten Speed Press team, especially Emma Campion, Ashley Lima, Ashley Pierce, Windy Dorresteyn, Daniel Wikey, Heather Porter, and Dan Myers for their talents and for making a first-time author feel welcome at her first meeting. And to my editor, Julie Bennett, for her enthusiasm, insightful comments, and commitment to making my vision for Look Big better.

Thank you to the dozens of generous experts I interviewed, quoted and not. Thank you to the San Francisco Writers' Grotto, specifically Caroline Paul (for both asking the best questions and knowing all the answers) and Rodes Fishburne (for routinely checking in with a "What animal are you on?" You kept me going when I was only on crows). Thank you to Jasmine Wade for checking the facts.

Thank you, contributors, for so willingly and brilliantly sharing your tales. Thank you to the very rigorous Guerneville/Inverness Writers' Retreats, to the Anchovy Club for little fishes and lots of book knowledge, and to George McCalman and Greg Clarke, whose early input was invaluable. Thank you to my bestest friends on both coasts, including one in Namibia who suggested we take a "cheetah walk" (no thank you).

Thanks to Skarli Pena for everything. To Ida Richter for reading. To Cousin Dave and Ricki for eating. And to Mike Herzlinger for carrying the bear spray. Thank you to my sister, Julie Levin Herzlinger, who understands the perils of an otherwise peaceful walk in Bhutan. Thank you, always, to my father, Danny, who fears nothing but cruise ships, and to my mother, Margie, whose cat phobia probably somehow started all of this.

Thank you, Hazel, my little coauthor, and Oren, my little "lover of all creatures"—may you always be. I'm sorry for so many ants in your cereal. And, finally, thank you to Josh, who can spot a moose in the dark from a mile away, and whose love, support, and wise edits mean the world.

INDEX

A
allergies, 28, 59
alligators, 10–11, 140
ants, 12–14

B
bats, 17
bears, 7, 8, 18, 20–22, 140
bed bugs, 24, 27
bees, 28–29, 140
bison, 8, 31
black widow spiders, 32–33, 140
boars, wild, 132–34
bobcats, 34–35
Borel, Brooke, 27
bunnies, 94–96

C
car accidents, 51, 81
cockroaches, 37–39
Colin, Chris, 45
cougars. See mountain lions
cows, 41, 140
coyotes, 8, 42–43, 45, 140
crows, 46–48

D
deer, 51–52, 84, 127, 140
dogs, 55, 92, 118, 140
donkeys, 56–57
dust mites, 59

E
E. coli, 40, 67
elephant seals, 60–61

F
Fish, Peter, 22
foxes, 63
fruit flies, 64
Funk, McKenzie, 14

G
geese, 66–67
great horned owls, 88–89
grizzlies, 7, 18, 20–22

H
hornets, 28–29, 140
horses, 68–69, 140
Hua, Vanessa, 52

J
jaguars, 71
jellyfish, 72–73

K
Kapp, Diana, 106

L
lice, 74–75
Lyme disease, 126, 127

M
malaria, 82
Marx, Rebecca Flint, 96
mice, 76–78, 127
moose, 7, 80–81
mosquitoes, 17, 82–83
mountain lions (cougars), 8, 35, 84–85, 92, 140

N

Nosrat, Samin, 78

O

opossums, 86–87
Orner, Peter, 100
owls, 88–89

P

pigeons, 90–91
pigs, wild, 132–34
porcupines, 92
Portuguese man-of-war, 72, 73

R

rabbits, 94–96
rabies, 17, 55, 87, 98
raccoons, 8, 98, 100
rats, 102–4, 106
rattlesnakes, 108–9, 140

S

salmonella, 67, 102
seagulls, 110–11
seals, 60–61
sea urchins, 112–13
sharks, 40, 72, 114–17, 140
sheep, 118–19
skunks, 89, 121
snakes, 40, 108–9, 140
spiders, 32–33, 140
squirrels, 122–23
stingrays, 125

T

tetanus, 55
ticks, 51, 126–27
Tsui, Bonnie, 38
turkeys, 128–29

W

wasps, 28–29, 140
West Nile virus, 82
whales, 130–31
wolves, 136, 140
woodpeckers, 138–39

For Josh, who's always scanning.

Text copyright © 2018 by Rachel Levin
Illustrations copyright © 2018 by Jeff Östberg

All rights reserved.
Published in the United States by Ten Speed Press, an imprint of the Crown Publishing Group, a division of Penguin Random House LLC, New York.
www.crownpublishing.com
www.tenspeed.com

Ten Speed Press and the Ten Speed Press colophon are registered trademarks of Penguin Random House LLC.

Library of Congress Cataloging-in-Publication Data is on file with the publisher.

Paperback ISBN: 978-0-399-58037-6
eBook ISBN: 978-0-399-58038-3

Printed in China

Design by Ashley Lima

10 9 8 7 6 5 4 3 2 1

First Edition

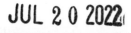